# Joy
## in Confession

Reclaiming Sacramental Reconciliation

# Praise for *Joy in Confession*

*Our campus ministry has everyone from devout Roman Catholics and passionate Protestants to cradle Episcopalians and reticent seekers, and Hillary Raining's book has something important to teach each and every one of us. I am grateful for this treatment of an oft-neglected rite that has such profound implications for the ministry of reconciliation given by Christ to the Church. Priests and parishioners, young and old, will find a beautiful resource for deepening Christian spirituality through the restorative practice of joyful confession.*

**The Rev. Chad Sundin, OSBCn**
Episcopal Campus Ministries
Arizona State University

*Reading* Joy in Confession *with a group of parishioners was a rich experience for all of us as we delved into the history and theology of confession and then into our need for confession and reconciliation. A number of those who participated in the group availed themselves of the sacrament during Holy Week.* Joy in Confession *worked perfectly for a Lenten book study, and I'm sure I will use this book again, both in a book group and as the basis for a retreat. I also plan to keep extra copies on my shelf to hand out to those who come to me with questions about guilt, forgiveness, and reconciliation. This is a great resource for individuals too!*

**The Rev. E. Suzanne Wille**
The Episcopal Church of All Saints
Indianapolis, Indiana

Joy in Confession *is an outstanding explanation of reconciliation and the need for it. The book equipped people at our church with a better understanding of confession as a sacrament in the Episcopal spiritual toolbox.*

**The Rev. Anjel Scarborough**
Grace Episcopal Church
Brunswick, Maryland

*Hillary Raining has created a resource with pastoral sensitivity, a practical knowledge born of her own parish experience and an abiding love for scripture and tradition. This book quickly opened up a conversation in our parish about confession, a topic long held in the silence of misconceptions and embarrassment. The brevity and clarity of the chapters appealed to a wide audience while the reflections, exercises, and liturgies gave the leader ample tools and flexibility to adapt the resource to the local context. Parishioners continue to mention concepts learned in our study; it is exciting to see the book plant seeds for ongoing conversation and Christian formation. I would consider using the activities and chapters in upcoming confirmation studies with teenagers as well as future conversations with individuals and small groups.*

**The Rev. Jennifer Zogg**
Church of the Epiphany
Providence, Rhode Island

*This style of study is a bit outside of my box—I don't normally incorporate art projects into Bible study—but I found this style of learning worked really well for parishioners. It made me realize that I should do more of this! Hillary's approach to a sometimes difficult topic was exactly what our congregation needed to explore confession and what it means to be a genuine Christian community.*

**The Rev. Rob Courtney**
St. Paul's Episcopal Church
New Orleans, Louisiana

# Joy
## in Confession

Reclaiming Sacramental Reconciliation

Hillary D. Raining

FORWARD MOVEMENT
Cincinnati, Ohio

Cover photo graciously offered by Jason Sierra and used with permission.

*Praying With the Body: Bringing the Psalms to Life.*
Copyright 2009 © Roy DeLeon. Used by permission
of Paraclete Press, www.paracletepress.org.

Psalms are from *The Book of Common Prayer*, unless noted.

Scripture quotations are from the New Revised Standard Version
Bible, © 1989 by National Council of the Churches of Christ in the
United States of America. Used by permission. All rights reserved.

*Living In the Green*, The Beecken Center of the School of Theology
at the University of the South. Co-authored by Courtney V. Cowart
and James M. Goodmann. Used with permission.
www.programcenter.sewanee.edu/programs/living-in-the-green.

ISBN: 9780880284455

Forward
Movement

# Table of Contents

# A Word from the Author

**"C**onfession??? We're not going to have to do that here, are we? That kind of stuff is why I left the Catholic Church!" This comment greeted me after I preached a sermon on the importance of reconciliation and confession. Although it was not the kind of remark I hoped to hear, it was not wholly unexpected. After all, I have never heard people say that private confession was their favorite thing about church!

Every time I talk about the Rite of Reconciliation of a Penitent—often thought of as "private confession"—I receive a host of reactions, ranging from the supportive to the downright defiant. So, I wasn't surprised by such strong emotions surrounding the topic of confession greeting me at the church door after my sermon. Yet what astonished me—and still does—is just how many people are unaware that private confession exists in the Episcopal Church. And when they discover that it does, people often have a lot to say about it—a few good things, but mostly negative.

Confession gets a bad rap. It sounds like it's full of judgment, a calculated litany of our own shortcomings. But the rite of confession in the Episcopal Church can offer deep joy and spiritual rebirth. I have personally experienced both new life from the practice of the Rite of Reconciliation as well as what can happen when the reconciliation rite is not an option.

When I was young, I felt drawn to the idea of confession. My Episcopal church didn't offer the rite, so I tried a Roman Catholic church. (I actually skipped school to do so, which I had to add to the list of sins I was preparing to confess!)

Unfortunately, the Roman Catholic priest, upon hearing that I was an Episcopalian, ordered me to leave. This refusal was a crushing blow: It felt as though I was not even worth listening to, let alone worthy to be forgiven. It was as if God was telling me that I was so immoral that nothing I had to say mattered, even "I'm sorry." I left the church in tears and took a seat on a nearby park bench. After sobbing for a long time, I suddenly remembered all the times that I had heard God's forgiveness and care for me in my Episcopal church. I decided that perhaps the priest's reaction was more about *his* unwillingness to see me as a child of God than *God's* unwillingness. Resolved, I made my confession to an Episcopal priest (after he told me that it was an option in our tradition). And I experienced tremendous joy. I was heard, my story was treated as sacred, and I listened in turn to the story of God's forgiveness and love as pardon was given.

Reconciliation is one of the most beautiful and life-changing gifts that Jesus offers us. It is also one of the most misunderstood. This book has its grounding in both my experiences as a person of faith and as a priest, as well as in my doctoral thesis that began with the question: Why do Episcopal churches frequently fail to offer and promote the Rite of Reconciliation—and what would happen if they did? The same question is valid for individuals: Why do we shy away from this beautiful gift, and what would happen if we took confession—and its promise of new life—seriously? My research showed that people's lives were changed when they were introduced to, guided in, and given the opportunity to experience some form of reconciliation.

This resource provides a user-friendly, hands-on model to embrace and explore reconciliation for churches and individuals. It combines art therapy, scholarship, theology, and worship to create a powerful experience for all. My prayer is that you will be enriched by delving deeper into this often misunderstood gem of the Episcopal tradition. Indeed, I hope that you will feel called to make a confession and experience the joy that it brings. This book will give you all the tools you need to prepare your heart as well as to live into your reconciliation with God.

The Rite of Reconciliation holds a key to grace and an invitation from God to live with joy as a people of a resurrected hope, if we would but answer the call.

May God's peace be with you.

**Hillary D. Raining**

~ ~ ~

**A special note of thanks** to congregations and communities that previewed *Joy in Confession* and offered invaluable feedback:

✢ The Episcopal Church of All Saints, Indianapolis, Indiana; the Rev. E. Suzanne Wille

✢ Grace Episcopal Church, Brunswick, Maryland; the Rev. Anjel Scarborough

✢ Church of the Epiphany, Rumford, Rhode Island; the Rev. Jennifer Zogg

✢ St. Paul's Episcopal Church, New Orleans, Louisiana; the Rev. Rob Courtney

✢ St. David's Episcopal Church, Radnor, Pennsylvania; the Rev. W. Frank Allen

✢ Episcopal Campus Ministries at Arizona State University; the Rev. Chad Sundin

✢ St. Christopher's Episcopal Church, Gladwyne, Pennsylvania, where I am honored to serve as rector

✢ My wonderfully supportive husband Ken and our bright light, Delia.

# Using this Resource

This workbook can be used by individuals (either alone or in a spiritual direction setting) or by faith communities looking to help members incorporate the principles and practice of the Rite of Reconciliation into their lives. Indeed, this tool was intentionally designed so that it can be used in various settings, so feel free to use it in ways that make sense for your setting. Some suggestions for group use include:

✣ An adult book study that meets during educational time on a Sunday or during the week.

✣ A weekend retreat

✣ A quiet day

✣ Confirmation class

✣ Teen groups or youth group retreat

✣ College chaplaincy groups

> Doodle in the margins. Take notes. Dog-ear pages. Make this book a companion on your journey to understanding the Rite of Reconciliation of a Penitent.

Leaders can incorporate the creative exercises as time allows. While the exercises promote a deeper understanding of the concepts contained in the book, feel free to leave out some elements, depending on the context or needs. However, don't omit an exercise simply because you or your group may not be accustomed to creative or artistic expressions and you worry that they (or you!) might not like the activities. Trying something new can promote a willingness to see the world in a different way. And remember that people respond to various learning styles. You should also feel free to supplement these discussions with anything you see fit to add.

If used in a group setting, all participants in the process should have a copy of the book as it provides space for reflection and an opportunity to revisit particular commentary.

This workbook is also an excellent pastoral tool. Every church should have a few copies on hand to distribute to individuals who are working through shame, guilt, or sin; considering making a confession; looking to grow in their spiritual life; or curious about the theological roots of confession. It is also a helpful tool to take to someone who is in the hospital and might have some hard questions to ask or decisions to make.

The Appendix includes additional resources to help facilitate individual reflection, group discussion, retreats, and worship. Worksheet pages for each chapter are included in the "Resources for Participants" section of the Appendix. The Appendix also includes resources for priests to become more familiar with the sacramental rite and to invite the congregation to experience joy in confession.

# Introduction

The need for reconciliation is tremendous. All we need to do is look around us, watch the news, read social media, and talk with friends and neighbors to see brokenness in the world. We are surrounded by people and situations that put distance and space between us rather than bring us together. Systems of shame and guilt hedge us in from every side. We live in an era where people have more virtual friends than true communities, a time that so often seems devoid of peace and love. Sin seems to be winning.

Yet, it doesn't have to be this way.

As Christians, we know the great joy that God has given us through the reconciling work of Jesus Christ. We know that God extends to us the invitation to live as new creations and to make the world around us a place of abundant life. Reconciliation is not simply the hope that things will be better or that they will somehow be joined in harmony. Reconciliation is nothing less than bringing all of creation—our lives and the world—back to God so that we might live, truly live. Reconciliation is an invitation to resurrection, not only in the world to come but also in our world here and now. Reconciliation is the work of the Church, and it has the power to change everything.

Through my research and experience, I have found that people and churches who practice the Rite of Reconciliation experience:

- ✥ Closer relationships with God
- ✥ The fulfillment of our natural desire for connection—both with God and with others

- ✛ Feelings of being heard and valued

- ✛ The possibility to live longer and healthier lives

- ✛ True and life-changing forgiveness

- ✛ A church that is a true public witness of confessing our sins and embracing forgiveness

- ✛ Places where true connection and community are valued and offered

- ✛ Churches that truly live into their missions to become the incarnation of God's word made flesh

Sounds great! How do we get started? Let's begin with understanding what we mean by the gift of new life through reconciliation. After all, before we can offer this gift to others, we must experience what it means to accept and practice reconciliation ourselves.

> At its heart, reconciliation is the very cornerstone of our faith—the love of God proclaimed in the forgiveness and healing offered to us by Jesus.

## Reconciliation of a Penitent: What Is It?

The theological explanation of reconciliation is both complicated and simple. At its heart, reconciliation is the very cornerstone of our faith—the love of God proclaimed in the forgiveness and healing offered to us by Jesus. We often hear the phrases "Jesus died for our sins" or "Jesus died to save you." Yet, understanding how that forgiveness works in our day-to-day life can be difficult. The Rite of Reconciliation exists so that we can live into the forgiving action of Jesus as found in his Body, the community of the Church, and as people of God.

Look at the words in the Rite of Reconciliation of a Penitent as outlined in *The Book of Common Prayer* on pages 447-452.

- ✛ **Penitent:** A person who has repented of his or her sins and is seeking the forgiveness of God.

✢ **Reconciliation:** This refers to the joy of being reunited and brought back into a right relationship and knowledge of God's love and forgiveness. In Christ we believe that God has reconciled all of creation to God's self and desires that all should be made one. The opportunity to change one's heart, mind, and behavior, and then accept God's forgiveness is at the very core of salvation. It represents the renewal of creation that is inaugurated by the resurrection of Jesus.

✢ **Reconciliation of a Penitent:** In the Episcopal tradition, it "is the rite in which those who repent of their sins may confess them to God in the presence of a priest, and receive the assurance of pardon and the grace of absolution." It is often referred to as "private confession."

What does that mean? Reconciliation invites us to leave our tombs (our sins and failings) and live the life God calls us to. Reconciliation means we become one again with our Lord and Savior—that we experience the Easter promise of new life.

When people truly embrace and practice Reconciliation of a Penitent, they will be transformed—as will the world around them.

✢ **Absolution of Sins:** The declaration made by the priest at the end of a confession to announce that the penitent is released from sin and is reminded that he or she is made a new creation. It is the moment when God's promised forgiveness is celebrated!

✢ **Confessor:** A Christian (usually a priest) serves as the listener to a private confession. Although all Christians may hear the confession of another person, only a priest may declare absolution.

✢ **Sin:** "Sin is the seeking of our own will instead of the will of God, thus distorting our relationship with God, with other people, and with all creation. Sin has power over us because we lose our liberty when our relationship with God is distorted" (*The Book of Common Prayer*, p. 848). In other words, sins include the actions that we do on our own that cause people harm. And sin is found in the broken systems of society as well as on a cosmic level. It can be helpful to think of this distinction between our personal and collective sins as "sins" with a lowercase s and the cosmic "Sin" with a capital "S." Personal sins are symptomatic of the power of Sin, and collective personal sins driven by the power of Sin become larger symptomatic/social sins. Yet, through our baptism, we have been given the power by God to break that system and cycle, and we can turn from Sin and sins and be forgiven through the repentance and forgiveness found in the Rite of Reconciliation.

✣ **Repentance:** This word literally means "to turn." It is associated with a spiritual desire to turn from habits, choices, or thoughts that lead us away from God.

✣ **Redemption:** "Redemption is the act of God which sets us free from the power of evil, sin, and death" (*The Book of Common Prayer*, p. 849). It is the saving action of Jesus on the cross and his liberating triumph over the grave in his resurrection—we often hear this as Christ "redeeming us from the grave." He gave his own life so that we would not have to taste eternal death, and it is this redemption that we are assured of during the absolution in the Rite of Reconciliation of a Penitent.

✣ **Grace:** "Grace is God's favor toward us, unearned and undeserved; by grace God forgives our sins, enlightens our minds, stirs our hearts, and strengthens our wills" (*The Book of Common Prayer*, p. 858). Grace is God's gift to us—the ultimate blessing in our lives.

✣ **Private/Auricular Confession:** This is another term for the sacramental rite known as Reconciliation of a Penitent.

4

- ✣ **Corporate/General Confession:** This refers to times when a group of Christians confess their sins and receive absolution as one body. Typically, corporate or general confession occurs before Holy Communion as a preparation to receive the sacrament.

- ✣ **The Seal of Confession:** Priests have an absolute duty to keep the seal of the confessional—that is, they are not to disclose anything that they learn during the course of Reconciliation of a Penitent. This is one of the most sacred and important duties for clergy.

## Why Churches and People Shy Away from Confession

Even this simple list of terms shows us the rich spiritual and theological implications of the Rite of Reconciliation. The glossary also reveals that the practice can be confusing, scary, and anxiety-producing. The Rite of Reconciliation dives right into the deepest and perhaps darkest parts of our soul and asks us to speak the truth we find there—and to another person no less! Sure, the idea of practicing the Rite of Reconciliation sounds good on paper. Who wouldn't want their sins to be forgiven and to be filled with the love and peace of Christ? Sounds great! So what's stopping us?

In my research and conversations, several factors appear to be stumbling blocks for both the Church and for individuals. These include:

- ✣ **Being unfamiliar with the rite** as an Episcopal service. The majority of Episcopalians do not know that confession is part of our tradition. It's pretty hard to use something if no one ever told you it exists!

- ✣ **Lingering resentment or trauma** from being required to make confessions in other denominations, including the Roman Catholic tradition. Others see the rite as too Roman Catholic—and not Protestant enough. Additionally, former members of some Evangelical denominations view sin and forgiveness (or lack thereof) as concepts that corrupt pastors have used to exert power over their followers.

✣ **Lack of education and understanding** about the rite. Many people who voice opposition to the rite say that they prefer to confess their sins directly to Christ, not to a priest whom they perceive as an intermediary between themselves and Jesus. In the Episcopal tradition, a personal relationship with Jesus is highly valued, but so too is the rich tradition of these sacramental rites passed down through the church for generations as a vehicle for Christ-centered relationships.

✣ **A societal drift** from people seeking spiritual health to primarily seeking psychological help. Again, the Episcopal Church is a denomination that values psychological therapy and the healing it can bring. Yet the Rite of Reconciliation offers renewal and healing for the soul. While therapy is a good and healthy thing for many, a familiarity with pop psychology has led some to search for solely scientific solutions to spiritual pains. Reconciliation seeks to paint a fuller picture of wholeness and healing. Forgiveness, which is beyond any therapist's diagnosis, is offered as a path to laying down the bonds of sin and choosing a new reality with God.

✣ **Cultural shift** and unwillingness to take responsibility for our actions. For example, anyone who has ever read the comment section on an Internet post has seen how we are living in a culture where people feel free to say terrible things about others, all the while protected by the anonymity of the web. These cruel comments can do huge damage to individuals and communities.

✜ **Clergy who are uncomfortable** with the rite due to lack of training or understanding or incorrectly viewing confession as a fringe ministry reserved only for highly liturgical churches. Some clergy might also worry that offering confession will create a perception that the church is judgmental.

Beyond these reasons that people and communities listed for why they felt unsure about Reconciliation of a Penitent, two underlying issues kept surfacing.

1. People felt that their sins were so bad that **they were not worthy** of seeing such a profound healing.

2. **They were embarrassed or ashamed** to share their sins with anyone else—even their priest.

Since these two factors were so prominent, we should take time to unpack them a bit.

## Unworthiness

Almost without exception, every person I spoke with—during my research and in continuing conversations as a parish priest—discussed feelings of unworthiness as a reason they did not seek reconciliation. Many of us have a hard time believing that God will forgive our sins—even after hearing over and over again that God will and does. One woman summed up this sentiment: "I know God will forgive my sins, but I don't think he should because they are just too terrible. And even if he does, I'll probably just end up doing it again."

These feelings were so prevalent, in fact, that I began to wonder if we were more Lenten people than Easter people. By that, I mean, do we find it easier to believe that we are cursed sinners and fundamentally bad people (a sentiment that seems more appropriate for the penitential season of Lent) than beloved children of God who have already been forgiven through the reconciling actions of Jesus' death and resurrection (the very thing we celebrate in Eastertide)?

This feeling of unworthiness is based on an assumption that we can keep God from loving us. With this view, we treat our sin as more powerful than God! According to theologian Malcolm C. Young, the problem of not fully understanding the Rite of Reconciliation may have its roots in the brokenness that all humanity bears: sin. He writes, "At a basic level, we are confused about what sin is, and as a result how we ought to seek reconciliation….We tend to mistakenly regard the violation [secularly and not biblically defined] as primary and its effect on our relationship to God as secondary, as if we have done something wrong and this has damaged our relationship to God."[1]

In other words, we tend to think of sin as the sum of things that we do, big and small, that keep us from the love of God. If we are good, God will love us. If we are bad, God shouldn't or won't love us. But to believe that individual sins can separate Christians from the love of God is to accept as truth that something about ourselves is inherently evil and wrong. If we start to see this as our reality, then we begin imagining our center as rooted in evil. That kind of worldview can mean the difference between saying, "I got angry and yelled at my kids. I was tired, but that doesn't make it right. Please forgive me, "and saying "I got angry and yelled at my kids because I'm a terrible person. I should have never had kids. I'll probably mess them up too."

Yes, sin causes us to lose our true north in Jesus, but there is nothing that can separate Christians from the forgiving love of God—least of all our actions as finite beings. As Paul tells us in Romans 8:38-39, "Neither death, nor life, nor angels, nor rulers, nor things present, nor things to come, nor powers, nor height, nor depth, nor anything else in all creation, will be able to separate us from the love of God in Christ Jesus our Lord." Paul is saying is that the grace God offers humanity in reconciliation breaks the cycle of our sin. We can actually let go of the sin—be truly done with it—with the help of Jesus. God doesn't love and forgive us because of how good we are. God loves and forgives us because of how good God is. Reconciliation invites us to embrace that reality and never look back.

> God doesn't love and forgive us because of how good we are. God loves and forgives us because of how good God is.

## Embarrassment and Shame

Another worry that keeps people away from confession is the difficulty of speaking to another person about the things you have done wrong. Because of the vulnerability that this requires, private confession has developed the reputation of being scary, uncomfortable, and shameful. This response is especially poignant for those who come from traditions where confession has been used to increase feelings of shame. Indeed, when the Rite of Reconciliation is administered inappropriately, it can be traumatic. If a person is worried that the all-important "seal of confession" (the priest's vow of complete and total confidentiality) might be broken, then they are very unlikely to feel safe enough to make a full confession. Violations of the seal of confession can take many forms. For example, a priest might try to continue the conversation about the confession at another time, which could amplify feelings of shame and guilt even after they have been forgiven. Or a priest might tell others about the confession, which would be grounds for that priest to be defrocked (dismissed from the priesthood). In addition, the priest may be overly judgmental or shaming while he or she hears the confession. The potential for spiritual trauma is especially present in the rite since the priest offers (or could withhold) absolution on behalf of the church in the name of God. To be rejected in such a moment, when you are emotionally and spiritually vulnerable, can be catastrophic to feelings of self-worth.

Some people worry that their confessions will change their relationship with the confessor. They fear that their clergy person might think less of them after hearing their confession or that it could sour a good relationship. Again, a good confessor is bound to keeping the seal of confession—essentially, what happens in confession stays in confession. That means the relationship outside of the Rite of Reconciliation should not change.

Still, the fear of judgment is ever-present for many when considering confession and absolution. A major criticism of Christianity is that it is often seen as judgmental—criticizing others for acts it deems unsuitable or unworthy. No one wants to be judged. Of course, in a sense, there is judgment of sin in confession, simply naming that sin is sin. The difference in this type of judgment is that it is followed by forgiveness, by the opportunity to be reconciled to our loving God and to start anew. That is the grace of God.

If we desire a life lived as the true children of God that we are called to be, we need to take an honest look at our sins. Otherwise, we carry things around in our souls that we are judging as wrong.

Feelings of unworthiness and shame share a common trait—a lack of Christ-like vulnerability. Author Brené Brown in her book, *Daring Greatly,* defines vulnerability as "uncertainty, risk, and emotional exposure"—all things that people might reasonably associate with doing something as honest and revealing as a private confession. After all, when you speak the truth about your actions and decisions, you have to be prepared to face your own brokenness. In order to do such a brave thing as confess your sin to someone else, you have to know that it is a safe place to do such a thing— that strict confidentiality will be kept, that you will be met

> Far from being judgmental when hearing a confession, clergy feel honored to make room for the sacred story. In fact, many clergy speak of a "holy forgetting" that happens after hearing a confession—by this they mean that they truly do not remember the details of the confession but have given it fully to God. Clergy are also blessed by you: During the rite, clergy will ask your prayers on his or her behalf, as sinners in God's sight.

with love and acceptance, and that you will be given the joy of forgiveness. All these elements can be found in the Rite of Reconciliation when administered by a good confessor.

## Confession as Connection

One of the great gifts of private confession is that it connects us not only with God but also with another human being. This gift of connection is very important as we are creatures who long for deep relationship. Indeed, we know from scientific research that the human brain is hardwired for connection. Research by the University of York "suggests that the number and quality of a person's social connections affect specific measures of health over the course of a lifetime. Older adults who feel socially isolated are more than twice as likely to develop high blood pressure, making loneliness a more significant risk factor for the condition than diabetes…Loneliness is also very bad for the heart. Social ties are also critical early on in life. Lonely teens, for example, are as likely to develop inflammation as young people who are sedentary…and for all age groups, social connections mitigate the harmful effects of daily stress."[2]

If the need to connect with other people is strong, how much stronger is the desire for deep connection with God? The Rite of Reconciliation offers a spiritual tool for connecting with God and with others by giving a living, breathing human to truly listen.

The irony of Reconciliation of a Penitent's bad reputation is that, while there is a need for emotional exposure, there is no shame in the rite. In his death, Jesus took upon himself all death—that means that he took our sins, and he took our shame. His desire to reconcile us to himself was so strong that he gave his life to bring us into right relationship with him. When we come to God with an earnest desire to know God's love and to be reconciled with

> In his death, Jesus took upon himself all death—that means that he took our sins, and he took our shame.

God, we will be welcomed. No other relationship, covenant, bond, or institution offers such certainty. And the priest, as God's ambassador for the Rite of Reconciliation, is a symbol of the love and connection that God desires for the Church and God's people. The priest hears these sacred stories and then hands them over to God—vowing to never break the bond of confidentiality that comes with such a responsibility of office.

Furthermore, the priest is standing as a symbol of the Christian family as a whole. Being a follower of Jesus means that you never have to suffer alone. You can call on your community in times of need—and that includes spiritual needs. We see that in James 5:13-16, we read, "Are any among you suffering? They should pray. Are any cheerful? They should sing songs of praise. Are any among you sick? They should call for the elders of the church and have them pray over them, anointing them with oil in the name of the Lord. The prayer of faith will save the sick, and the Lord will raise them up; and anyone who has committed sins will be forgiven." Notice that forgiveness of sins, far from being something shameful, is one of the very things the church community is called to do for her members. You might ask: "What would such a community look like if we really lived into that call?"

When practiced with care and sacred listening, Reconciliation of a Penitent gives us the ultimate safe space to bring shame to its knees and make our churches these safe places. In this sacramental act, participants are invited to speak the truth about sin and called to leave the burden of those sins there, in that moment. Once we have repented and, with God's help, are resolved to walk away from that sin and back to God, we are forgiven. We are reconciled with God and nothing else can offer such freedom, joy, and purpose of life. It is true grace.

> When Christians take part in confession, they join God in the creative act of speaking the Word into flesh.

Finally, perhaps the most important gift of the Rite of Reconciliation is how it makes peace and love manifest in our lives. The centrality of the incarnation—that the Word became flesh to live and die as one of us—points to the importance of actually speaking aloud the need for reconciliation that happens in the confessional moment. Just as new life and peace have been given to us through the Word of God and the Holy Spirit, so too is new life made an embodied reality simply by giving voice to our old ways. To that end, theologian L. Gregory Jones writes, "when the resurrected Christ returns to his frightened and bewildered disciples, he again says, 'Receive the Holy Spirit. If you forgive anyone's sins, they are forgiven. If you retain anyone's sins, they are retained' (John 20:21-23). There is thus an inextricable relationship between receiving the Holy Spirit and engaging in practices of forgiveness. Indeed, the Spirit works both to turn and re-turn people to the power of Christ's forgiveness and to embody that forgiveness in relations with others. One cannot be had without the other."[3] In other words, when Christians take part in confession, they join God in the creative act of speaking the Word into flesh. Conversely, when Christians hear the words of forgiveness, peace and love are made manifest.

In the chapters that follow, we will delve deeper into the healing, pastoral, and Easter-centered gift of the Rite of Reconciliation. We will find new pathways to transformation, truly living as the new creations and ambassadors of love and light that we are called to be by God. It is the hope that this book will help you feel called to seek joy and embrace the practice of private confession, the Rite of Reconciliation of a Penitent.

# 1

# Reconciliation in the Bible and in *The Book of Common Prayer*

*So if anyone is in Christ, there is a new creation: everything old has passed away; see, everything has become new! All this is from God, who reconciled us to himself through Christ, and has given us the ministry of reconciliation; that is, in Christ God was reconciling the world to himself, not counting their trespasses against them, and entrusting the message of reconciliation to us. So we are ambassadors for Christ, since God is making his appeal through us; we entreat you on behalf of Christ, be reconciled to God. For our sake he made him to be sin who knew no sin, so that in him we might become the righteousness of God.*

—2 CORINTHIANS 5:17-21

# Opening Prayer

O God, whose glory it is always to have mercy: Be gracious to all who have gone astray from your ways, and bring them again with penitent hearts and steadfast faith to embrace and hold fast the unchangeable truth of your Word, Jesus Christ your Son; who with you and the Holy Spirit lives and reigns, one God, for ever and ever. **Amen.**

—*THE BOOK OF COMMON PRAYER*, p. 218

# The Biblical Roots of Reconciliation

Now that we have talked about the Rite of Reconciliation of a Penitent, you might be wondering how it came into practice. After all, we have a personal advocate with God through Jesus. So why do we have a rite that involves another person or the Church? To answer this question, let's start with the scriptural roots of reconciliation. The opening message of the Gospel of Mark, announced by John the Baptist, reiterated by Jesus, and finally proclaimed by the apostles, is "Repent, and believe in the good news" (1:15). In other words, seek reconciliation, turn back to God, and believe in Christ Jesus, the risen Lord. Jesus himself takes up this call to repentance as we see in verses such as Matthew 4:17 where he says, "Repent, for the kingdom of heaven has come near." Jesus clearly makes repentance a huge topic in his preaching and through his actions, both in life and in death, but he doesn't stop there. He also makes sure his disciples continue this reconciling work. In Matthew 16:13-19, Jesus discusses with his disciples the nature of his identity.

*Now when Jesus came into the district of Caesarea Philippi, he asked his disciples, "Who do people say that the Son of Man is?" And they said, "Some say John the Baptist, but others Elijah, and still others Jeremiah or one of the prophets." He said to them, "But who do you say that I am?" Simon Peter answered, "You are the Messiah, the Son of the living God." And Jesus answered him, "Blessed are you, Simon son of Jonah! For flesh and blood has not revealed this to you, but my Father in heaven. And I tell you, you are Peter, and on this rock I will build my church, and the gates of Hades will not prevail against it. I will give you the keys of the kingdom of heaven, and whatever you bind on earth will be bound in heaven, and whatever you loose on earth will be loosed in heaven."*

Key moments in this passage relate to the Rite of Reconciliation. First, Jesus asks his disciples who they say he is. This is no mere exercise in curiosity on Jesus' part. Remembering who Jesus is—God in human form—is an important first step in the process of reconciliation. In fact, you might even say it is the very nature of humility. When we are being humble, we are not feeling bad about ourselves. To be truly humble means that we are remembering who is God and who is not. And at that same moment, we remember that we are God's children and that we are created in God's image. We are both dust and divine light at the same time, and when we "humble ourselves" before Jesus as he asked the disciples to do, we recall this beautiful reality.

Secondly, Peter makes an actual confession in this story. When he is asked by Jesus squarely, "Who do you say that I am?", Jesus is asking Peter to be very real. He is, in essence, saying, *Put down any pretense; discard others' view of who I am and tell me who you say that I am.* Peter declares that Jesus is the Messiah—he declares the truth about life to the face of the One who is with us. When we engage in the Rite of Reconciliation, we are confessing the exact same thing. We are being real and honest with Jesus about who we think he is—he is the one who has promised to be with us and love us even when we have sinned.

Here's an important note about the word confess. I think many of us hear this word and automatically assume that we're talking about an admission of wrongdoing. That is, of course, one definition of confess, and it plays a key role in the Rite of Reconciliation, which is often called confession. But confess has another important meaning: to declare. So when we confess who Jesus is, we are declaring it—an echo of Peter's declaration.

Jesus tells Peter and the disciples that they are to carry out this ministry of forgiveness and declaration of pardon by saying that "whatever they bind on earth will be bound in heaven and whatever they loose on earth will be loosed in heaven." This verse is a cornerstone for the understanding of reconciliation in the life of the church: It reminds us that the disciples of Jesus are indeed the Body of Christ here and now. The church serves as the face of the love of God for us and as such, is privileged with the great joy of reminding people that they are forgiven.

As Paul seeks to follow Jesus' call to the disciples, he explores reconciliation in his second letter to the Corinthians. Paul expands on the nature of God's love and its implications for the Christian life, using powerful imagery to describe this ministry of reconciliation (5:17-21). Paul notes that those who seek to represent Christ are not merely bearers of good news. Instead he chooses the word "ambassador" to describe the work. In the Greek language in which Paul was writing, the term ambassador referred to someone who was directly representing the emperor. Such a person would be sent into an area to set up a system of government that would fall under the rule of the empire. The ambassadors would fulfill such duties as establishing boundaries, instituting a legal system, and drawing up new laws. So when Paul describes Christ's followers as ambassadors of Christ, he is saying that we are going into the world to set up something new, to create a new reality where people can dwell and live as reconciled people here and now. It's nothing short of creating a new world in Christ's name.

In the Episcopal Church, the biblical concept of reconciliation is most prominently lived out in baptism and in the liturgical rite, Reconciliation of the Penitent. As we explored in the introduction, at its core, the Rite of Reconciliation of a Penitent is about living out the biblical gift of repenting of our sins, confessing them to God, and receiving the grace of absolution—all of which has its grounding in the call of John the Baptist, Jesus, and the other New Testament writers.

> Reconciliation is so central to the Episcopal view of Christianity that it is the very core of the calling of each member and leader.

Through this biblical mandate, our rich liturgical tradition stands very much in relationship with the modern world. Indeed churches themselves are called to be centers of reconciliation. In fact, the core ministry of the laity and bishops as stated in *The Book of Common Prayer* "is to represent Christ and his church; to bear witness to him wherever they may be; and according to the gifts given to them, to carry on Christ's work of reconciliation in the world" (p. 855). In other words, reconciliation is so central to the Episcopal view of Christianity that it is the very core of the calling of each member and leader. We are to be Jesus' love to the world that so desperately needs to be brought back in relationship with God. In fact, I would go so far as to say that if churches are not centers where ambassadors of reconciliation can be trained or where people can come to find that renewal, then they are not being the Body of Christ and are not following their biblical mandate.

# Response

Ahelpful start to any journey is noting your starting point. That is very true in the reconciliation process. Take this time to write a letter to yourself. Include any fears, worries, hopes, or joys that may be on your heart. Do you have habits that have become stumbling blocks in your relationship with God or others? Be sure to mention who will be with you on this journey—or who you may need to avoid so that change can happen.

For your letter, you can use the space in the margins of this workbook, the worksheet in the Appendix (page 130), a journal, or fancy stationery. You decide what works best for you.

If you are in a group setting—and if you feel comfortable— share your reflections and listen to others' responses.

Another exercise in response to this chapter is to explore the two rites of Reconciliation of a Penitent offered in *The Book of Common Prayer* (pages 447-452). Both forms are included in the following pages.

You might also look at different reconciliation rites within the Christian tradition. Some good choices for comparison include: *The New Zealand Prayer Book, Evangelical Lutheran Worship, Iona Abbey Worship Book* (Celtic), and *Glory to God* (Presbyterian).

# The Reconciliation
# of a Penitent

**Form One**

*The Penitent begins*

Bless me, for I have sinned.

*The Priest says*

The Lord be in your heart and upon your lips that you may truly and humbly confess your sins: In the Name of the Father, and of the Son, and of the Holy Spirit. ***Amen***.

*Penitent*

I confess to Almighty God, to his Church, and to you, that I have sinned by my own fault in thought, word, and deed, in things done and left undone; especially _____. For these and all other sins which I cannot now remember, I am truly sorry. I pray God to have mercy on me. I firmly intend amendment of life, and I humbly beg forgiveness of God and his Church, and ask you for counsel, direction, and absolution.

*Here the Priest may offer counsel, direction, and comfort.*
*The Priest then pronounces this absolution*

Our Lord Jesus Christ, who has left power to his Church to absolve all sinners who truly repent and believe in him, of his great mercy forgive you all your offenses; and by his authority committed to me, I absolve you from all your sins: In the Name of the Father, and of the Son, and of the Holy Spirit. ***Amen***.

*or this*

Our Lord Jesus Christ, who offered himself to be sacrificed for us to the Father, and who conferred power on his Church to forgive sins, absolve you through my ministry by the grace of the Holy Spirit, and restore you in the perfect peace of the Church. ***Amen***.

The Lord has put away all your sins.

*Penitent*  Thanks be to God.

*The Priest concludes*

Go (or abide) in peace, and pray for me, a sinner.

*Declaration of Forgiveness to be used by a Deacon or Lay Person*

Our Lord Jesus Christ, who offered himself to be sacrificed for us to the Father, forgives your sins by the grace of the Holy Spirit. **Amen**.

~ ~ ~

## Form Two

*The Priest and Penitent begin as follows*

Have mercy on me, O God, according to your loving-kindness;
    in your great compassion blot out my offenses.
Wash me through and through from my wickedness,
    and cleanse me from my sin.
For I know my transgressions only too well,
    and my sin is ever before me.

Holy God, Holy and Mighty, Holy Immortal One,
    have mercy upon us.

*Penitent*  Pray for me, a sinner.

*Priest*

May God in his love enlighten your heart, that you may remember in truth all your sins and his unfailing mercy. **Amen**.

*The Priest may then say one or more of these or other appropriate verses of Scripture, first saying:*

Hear the Word of God to all who truly turn to him.

Come to me, all ye that travail and are heavy laden, and I will refresh you. *Matthew 11:28*

God so loved the world, that he gave his only-begotten Son, to the end that all that believe in him should not perish, but have everlasting life. *John 3:16*

This is a true saying, and worthy of all men to be received, that Christ Jesus came into the world to save sinners. *1 Timothy 1:15*

If any man sin, we have an Advocate with the Father, Jesus Christ the righteous; and he is the perfect offering for our sins, and not for ours only, but for the sins of the whole world. *1 John 2:1-2*

*The Priest then continues*
Now, in the presence of Christ, and of me, his minister, confess your sins with a humble and obedient heart to Almighty God, our Creator and our Redeemer.

*The Penitent says*
Holy God, heavenly Father, you formed me from the dust in your image and likeness, and redeemed me from sin and death by the cross of your Son Jesus Christ. Through the water of baptism you clothed me with the shining garment of his righteousness, and established me among your children in your kingdom. But I have squandered the inheritance of your saints, and have wandered far in a land that is waste.

Especially, I confess to you and to the Church…

*Here the Penitent confesses particular sins.*
Therefore, O Lord, from these and all other sins I cannot now remember, I turn to you in sorrow and repentance. Receive me again into the arms of your mercy, and restore me to the blessed company of your faithful people; through him in whom you have redeemed the world, your Son our Savior Jesus Christ. ***Amen***.

*The Priest may then offer words of comfort and counsel.*

*Priest*
Will you turn again to Christ as your Lord?

*Penitent*   I will.

*Priest*

Do you, then, forgive those who have sinned against you?

*Penitent*   I forgive them.

*Priest*

May Almighty God in mercy receive your confession of sorrow and of faith, strengthen you in all goodness, and by the power of the Holy Spirit keep you in eternal life. ***Amen***.

*The Priest then lays a hand upon the penitent's head (or extends a hand over the penitent), saying one of the following*

Our Lord Jesus Christ, who offered himself to be sacrificed for us to the Father, and who conferred power on his Church to forgive sins, absolve you through my ministry by the grace of the Holy Spirit, and restore you in the perfect peace of the Church. ***Amen***.

*or this*

Our Lord Jesus Christ, who has left power to his Church to absolve all sinners who truly repent and believe in him, of his great mercy forgive you all your offenses; and by his authority committed to me, I absolve you from all your sins: In the Name of the Father, and of the Son, and of the Holy Spirit. ***Amen***.

*The Priest concludes*

Now there is rejoicing in heaven; for you were lost, and are found; you were dead, and are now alive in Christ Jesus our Lord. Go (or abide) in peace. The Lord has put away all your sins.

*Penitent*   Thanks be to God.

*Declaration of Forgiveness to be used by a Deacon or Lay Person*

Our Lord Jesus Christ, who offered himself to be sacrificed for us to the Father, forgives your sins by the grace of the Holy Spirit. ***Amen***.

~ ~ ~

These two forms of private confession are found in the "Pastoral Office" section of *The Book of Common Prayer*. This section includes some of the most important rituals of our lives, such as confirmation, marriage, and burial. Martin L. Smith writes in his book, *Reconciliation: Preparing for Confession in the Episcopal Church*, that "Placing confession in this context makes an important point. Confession is one of the church's acts of worship. Although only two worshipers are present, they make up the necessary quorum for a meeting of the Christian community! (Matthew 18:20)…Confession is a service of worship, a meeting of the church in microcosm, with Christ active to reconcile and to heal." The beauty of this service of reconciliation is that it can be done any time and in any place with any other Christian. Although a priest is necessary to pronounce absolution through the offices of the church, anyone can remind us of the joyous news that we have been forgiven through Christ. Reconciliation of a Penitent should certainly be viewed as a pastoral gift that can be received by anyone, though no one need feel pressured to do so. Indeed, we have an expression in the church about who should partake in confession: "All may, some should, none must."

Form One and Form Two offer confessors a choice in how to shape their confession. The first is briefer and more direct; the second is longer, with more prayers and call-and-response between the confessor and the priest. Marion J. Hatchett notes in his book *Commentary on the American Prayer Book* that Form Two is a "much fuller form which is particularly appropriate when a person has turned or returned to the Christian faith, or at other possible 'crisis' points in a person's life." I have found that the first form, with its brevity, can be helpful when a person has spent a lot of time already thinking about confession and he or she needs to get the words out simply and directly. The confessor is told to "abide in peace," calling us to see the whole of our lives as the place where harmony can now reside. Notice that the priest also acknowledges his or her own sin and asks the newly reconciled for prayers of healing. This simple petition reminds us that the priest does not sit in judgment in this moment but serves as a companion in this Christian life.

For those who may need some help in finding the right words while making a confession, Form Two is an excellent choice with a powerful blend of scripture and baptismal allusions. In *Prayer Shapes Believing*, author Leonel L. Mitchell writes that Form Two is influenced by Eastern Orthodox tradition and "sets sin and forgiveness within the framework of the baptismal life in Christ" so we might continue to live united with him and his church. For example, Form Two begins with a "portion of Psalm 51, the great penitential psalm and the proclamation of the Gospel of salvation…This structure prevents us from thinking that it is our repentance which initiates reconciliation. From beginning to end reconciliation is the action of God, to whose call to repent we respond." In making our confession, we are responding to that holy action.

Both forms provide space for the priest and penitent to have pastoral conversation. Feel free to ask your priest any questions or share any concerns as she or he will likely have some words of counsel to offer. Your priest may also share some spiritual practices (such as a psalm, prayer, or hymn to be said or something to do) as a sign of penitence and as an act of thanksgiving. Since Jesus has already abolished sin in the work of the cross and resurrection, these acts of penitence are not to be seen as earning forgiveness but rather as tools to support your newly reconciled orientation.

# What to Expect
# When Making Confession

Although each location will be different according to your church's traditions and the style of your confessor, here are some things that you can expect when you make a confession. For more tips on how to prepare and process for a confession, please see Appendix B: Individual's Toolbox.

✣ Begin your journey to reconciliation with prayer and self-examination. Knowing that this opportunity is a call to grace and not a call to feel shame, ask God for clarity in those parts of your life that may need healing and change.

✣ When you feel the desire to seek reconciliation, call your church to make an appointment with your priest or make note of any previously scheduled times of confession that are posted in your church.

✣ The place where you make your confession will be confidential and sacred. Very few Episcopal churches have confessional booths; however if yours does, simply enter and either sit or kneel as the priest takes her or his place on the other side of the screen. If your church does not have a booth, you will mostly likely be invited to kneel at the altar rail or meet with the priest in his or her office. The confessor may sit facing you or in such a way as to not make direct eye contact with you; this may make the moment more comfortable for you and is a sign that your confessor is listening deeply on behalf of God.

✣ Using one of the reconciliation rites from *The Book of Common Prayer*, you will confess your sins and ask God for forgiveness. Don't worry if you can't remember everything! God knows what is on your heart.

✛ The priest may offer pastoral conversation and some spiritual practices (such as a psalm, prayer, or hymn to be said or something to do) to offer as a sign of penitence and an act of thanksgiving.

✛ The priest will then absolve you from your sins and remind you of the wonders of God's grace and forgiveness that you have received.

✛ Spend some time in prayer afterward to revel in the freedom and joy that God offers you in this pastoral gift of reconciliation.

# Reflection

The path of reconciliation is one of transformation. As you move further in your journey, it will be important to mark these changes to help you hear God's call for your recreated life. Answer the questions below to help explore your relationship with the Rite of Reconciliation during these first few sessions. If you are in a group setting—and if you feel comfortable—share your reflections and listen to others' responses. We will return to these questions at our last session to see what transformations may have taken place.

- ✛ Have you ever made a private confession? Why or why not?

- ✛ What does reconciliation mean to you?

- ✛ What is your understanding or hope of confession?

- ✛ What Bible story makes you think of forgiveness? Of confession?

- ✛ Have you had the experience of feeling guilty? Has that feeling led you to make a major change in your life? What was it? When did this happen?

- ✛ Why is it hard to ask for forgiveness?

- ✛ How much do you think sin weighs?

- ✛ Has shame ever prevented you from seeking forgiveness?

- ✛ How can you prepare yourself to take a step in the process of forgiveness?

# Closing

Today's prayer is based on traditional monastic prayers and can be practiced by individuals or groups. Volunteers may lead the prayers, read scripture, or other elements of the closing.

*If reading as a group, the bold indicates the group response.*

## Opening Prayer

Where you lead us, God,
> **let us follow.**

Holy God, you created us in your image and called us by our name. Be with us as we journey toward your grace and peace so that we can become the people you created us to be, free from that which blocks us from seeing ourselves clearly. **Amen.**

## Song of Praise

Arise, shine, for your light has come, *
> **and the glory of the Lord has dawned upon you.**

For behold, darkness covers the land; *
> **deep gloom enshrouds the peoples.**

But over you the Lord will rise, *
> **and his glory will appear upon you.**

Nations will stream to your light, *
> **and kings to the brightness of your dawning.**

Your gates will always be open; *
> **by day or night they will never be shut.**

They will call you, The City of the Lord, *
> **The Zion of the Holy One of Israel.**

Violence will no more be heard in your land, *
**ruin or destruction within your borders.**

You will call your walls, Salvation, *
**and all your portals, Praise.**

The sun will no more be your light by day; *
**by night you will not need the brightness
of the moon.**

The Lord will be your everlasting light, *
**and your God will be your glory.**

Glory to the Father, and to the Son, and to the Holy Spirit: *
**as it was in the beginning, is now, and will be
for ever. Amen.**

—SELECTIONS FROM ISAIAH 60

# Reading

So if anyone is in Christ, there is a new creation: everything
old has passed away; see, everything has become new! All
this is from God, who reconciled us to himself through Christ,
and has given us the ministry of reconciliation; that is, in
Christ God was reconciling the world to himself, not counting
their trespasses against them, and entrusting the message of
reconciliation to us. So we are ambassadors for Christ, since
God is making his appeal through us; we entreat you on behalf
of Christ, be reconciled to God.  For our sake he made him to
be sin who knew no sin, so that in him we might become the
righteousness of God.

–2 CORINTHIANS 5:17-21

# Reflection

Christ urges you, when you ask forgiveness for yourself, to be especially generous to others, so that your actions may commend your prayer.

—AMBROSE OF MILAN

✛ Who do you need to forgive?

✛ What do you need to be forgiven of?

*A moment of silence may be offered.*

# Confession

**Jesus, we lay before you all that we are carrying but can no longer bear the burden. We have hurt ourselves and others, and we have fallen short of the plans you have made for us. We confess these things now and ask for your forgiveness.**

# Assurance of Pardon

But while he was still far off, his father saw him and was filled with compassion; he ran and put his arms around him and kissed him.

–LUKE 15:20

# Prayers

*Offer prayers of thanksgiving, concern, or any other need.*

**The Lord's Prayer**

# Going out

Where you lead us, God,
**let us follow.**

# 2

# Sin

*I will give you the keys of the kingdom of heaven, and whatever you bind on earth will be bound in heaven, and whatever you loose on earth will be loosed in heaven.*

—MATTHEW 16:19

# Opening Prayer

Almighty God, you alone can bring into order the unruly wills and affections of sinners: Grant your people grace to love what you command and desire what you promise; that, among the swift and varied changes of the world, our hearts may surely there be fixed where true joys are to be found; through Jesus Christ our Lord, who lives and reigns with you and the Holy Spirit, one God, now and forever. **Amen.**

—*THE BOOK OF COMMON PRAYER*, P. 219

# The History of Sin

Almost since the beginning of time, we humans have had a problem. In a word: Sin. This book doesn't explore all of the complexities of theological thinking around the nature of sin. Indeed, sin, its effect on our lives, and the way God frees us from it, has spurred extensive volumes and countless debates and even denominational splits. Sadly, some theologians and church leaders have used the power of absolution and forgiveness of sins (or the withholding thereof) as a way to assert psychosocial and spiritual power over their congregants. Sin is a deep and loaded topic, and we won't reach a neat-and-tidy resolution about it here. However, it would be impossible to talk about reconciliation without mentioning that which we need to be reconciled back from—sin.

While specific actions can be sinful, our Episcopal understanding of sin is "the seeking of our own will instead of the will of God, thus distorting our relationship with God, with other people, and with all creation" (*The Book of Common Prayer*, p. 848). We see time and time again in scripture and, indeed, in the world around us, the disruption of these precious relational ties. We know these disruptions all too well—selfishness that causes us to care more about our own wants rather than others' needs; desires that lead us to stray from or betray our relationships; ways that we fail to care about creation or the generations that will come after us. We see this on a global scale with war, poverty, and racism. The way sin breaks our connections is a self-made reality that we live in every day. We should cherish these connections and this creation, but unfortunately we sacrifice them when we put our own desires before the will of God.

So why do we keep choosing to sin if the consequences are so obviously bad for us? Furthermore, how is sin even still possible since we have been taught that Jesus died for our sins? *The Book of Common Prayer* reminds us that "sin has power over us because we lose our liberty when our relationship with God is distorted" (p. 849). It may seem strange that by exercising our free will and choosing sin we actually lose our liberty. But we have a better understanding of this paradox when we place ourselves within the context of how sin works. Sin is not simply the actions that we do on our own that may cause harm. Sin is also found in the broken systems of society as well as on a cosmic level. It can be helpful to think of this distinction between our personal and collective sins as "sins" with a lowercase s and the cosmic sin that Paul talks about in Romans 5:20-6:14 as "Sin" with a capital S. Personal sins are symptomatic of the power of Sin, and collective personal sins driven by the power of Sin become larger symptomatic/social sins. Yet, through our baptism, we have been given the power by God to break that system.

> Through our baptism, we have been given the power by God to break the system of personal sin and cosmic Sin.

Paul reminds us that in his crucifixion, Jesus broke the power of that cosmic Sin by destroying death itself through his resurrection. In our baptisms, we are grafted into Jesus' death and resurrection. Thus, we too are no longer enslaved to sin or death—we are given the gift of being reconciled to God.

Paul describes this reconciliation in Romans 6:3-11:

> *Do you not know that all of us who have been baptized into Christ Jesus were baptized into his death? Therefore we have been buried with him by baptism into death, so that, just as Christ was raised from the dead by the glory of the Father, so we too might walk in newness of life. For if we have been united with him in a death like his, we will certainly be united with him in a resurrection like his. We know that our old self was crucified with him so that the body of sin might be destroyed, and we might no longer be enslaved to sin. For whoever has died is freed from sin. But if we have died with Christ, we believe that we will also live with him. We know that Christ, being raised from the dead, will never die again; death no longer has dominion over him. The death he died, he died to sin, once for all; but the life he lives, he lives to God. So you also must consider yourselves dead to sin and alive to God in Christ Jesus.*

Being a baptized Christian means that we have been so joined with Christ that we continually journey to grow into his "full stature" ( Ephesians 4:13). As we discuss in this chapter, Reconciliation of a Penitent gives us a way to address personal sins before they become a part of a systematic problem by confessing that Sin has no power over us through God's grace. It helps us to continue to live as people who have been freed from Sin.

Turning to our own Baptismal Covenant, we can see this pattern of cosmic, systematic, and personal sin as well as our public confession of renouncing it. Before people are baptized, they are asked questions that require them to leave the "death of sin" behind and proclaim their belief in Jesus' saving work of the cross and resurrection. These renunciations apply to both the personal sins and the big and cosmic Sin. Reconciliation begins with the personal sin and moves up through the system to reach the cosmic. It reinforces our baptismal identity.

These questions can be found in *The Book of Common Prayer* on page 302:

- ✛ Cosmic power of Sin ("Do you renounce Satan and all the spiritual forces of wickedness that rebel against God"?)

- ✛ Systemic sins of the world ("Do you renounce the evil powers of this world which corrupt and destroy the creatures of God?")

- ✛ Personal sinfulness ("Do you renounce all sinful desires that draw you from the love of God?")

- ✛ Then we confess a personal belief in Jesus as the one who saves us from all Sin/sin ("Do you turn to Jesus Christ and accept him as your Savior?")

With this understanding of personal and corporate sins being products of a cosmic Sin, we can begin to see how people have dealt with its effects throughout history. All too often, people equate sin and repentance with God being angry at us and wanting to punish us. We cling to a narrative that says we did something bad so God will demand retribution from us. The problem with this narrative and this view of sin is that it fails to remember that in Jesus, God has already "taken care" of Sin—on the cross, Jesus showed us God as both perfect judge and perfect grace. And although we may be uncomfortable with God as judge and prefer to hear about God's grace, we actually need both. We need God who looks at sinful things like pride, greed, and injustice and judges them as less than what the world should have. And we need a God who embodies the ultimate grace and gives us the means for our sinfulness to be healed and redeemed.

> On the cross, Jesus showed us God as both perfect judge and perfect grace.

Easy, right? If we simply follow in Jesus' way, we should be able to set sin aside and live lives that are more and more like

Jesus. We know, of course, that in reality, we keep sinning. We keep making decisions that move us out of relationship with God and others. We are selfish, forgetful, thoughtless, and mean-spirited—sometimes all at the same time! We keep doing things that draw us out of the lives that we were created to embody—lives that are peaceful, loving, and in union with God. Because of our propensity to sin, the Christian community has always had some form of Reconciliation of a Penitent. The history of sin and the church's understanding of both wrongdoing and repentance can be understood through the lens of the Rite of Reconciliation and how it has changed over the centuries.

Let's start at the beginning with the story of Cain and Abel. Now, you might have been expecting to start with the story of the Garden of Eden, since so much of what is popularly thought of as original sin has its roots within that story. However, as Everett Fox notes in *The Five Books of Moses*, the actual concept and word sin is not named in Genesis until the story of Cain's murder of his younger brother. In Genesis 4:1-16, Cain kills his younger brother after becoming angry when God disregards his sacrifice of grain in favor of Abel's offering of meat. Cain tries to cover up his actions when he is questioned by God about the fate of Abel ("I do not know: am I my brother's keeper?") and God hands down judgment (the soil which received his brother's blood will reject him, and he will be a wanderer on the earth). When Cain cries out that this punishment is too much for him to bear, he displays contrition. Even in the Hebrew Testament (where God often gets the unwarranted rap of being overly judgmental), God chooses to continue to be in relationship with Cain and protects him with a mark and a promise to stay with him. Cain goes on to have a family, and his descendants become skilled artisans and craftworkers, showing that there is redemption with God despite the most grievous of sins.

It's the beginning of a pattern that we humans will repeat

time and again—throughout scripture and today. God reaches out to redeem all people, to free us from our prideful ways, including making covenants with us (which we break), handing down the law to guide us (which we disobey), and sending prophets who call us to repent (who we ignore). To try to "make things right again" with God, people developed different rituals of reconciliation and repentance. One of the most notable examples in the Hebrew scriptures comes in the form of ritual animal sacrifice as a way of atonement. Although animal sacrifice seems very strange and even repugnant to our modern sensibilities, it was a very common religious practice in the time of the ancient Hebrews. Religious scholar William K. Gilders writes, "The English word 'sacrifice' comes from the Latin, *sacrifice*, 'to make sacred,' that is, to permanently transfer something from the human (common) realm to the divine/supernatural (sacred) realm."[4] The ancient Israelites viewed the location of God to be in the heavenly realms and the only way to transfer something to the heavens was to burn it, thereby turning the object into smoke that could ascend to God. These sacrifices were ways that people could call on God, and God would draw close to them.

The book of Leviticus in particular gives us a full outline of sin, purification, and guilt offerings that could be made when people sin and disrupt their relationship with God or their community. For example in Leviticus 6:1-7, we hear:

> The LORD spoke to Moses, saying: When any of you sin and commit a trespass against the LORD by deceiving a neighbor in a matter of a deposit or a pledge, or by robbery, or if you have defrauded a neighbor, or have found something lost and lied about it—if you swear falsely regarding any of the various things that one may do and sin thereby—when you have sinned and realize your guilt, and would restore what you took by robbery or by fraud or the deposit that was committed to you, or the lost thing that you found, or anything else about

*which you have sworn falsely, you shall repay the principal amount and shall add one-fifth to it. You shall pay it to its owner when you realize your guilt. And you shall bring to the priest, as your guilt-offering to the LORD, a ram without blemish from the flock, or its equivalent, for a guilt-offering. The priest shall make atonement on your behalf before the LORD, and you shall be forgiven for any of the things that one may do and incur guilt thereby.*

In this ritual of atonement, God gives the people a clear-cut way of restoring broken relationships. Not only is the infraction between neighbors corrected, but through the sacrifice of the ram, we proclaim the action of God to heal the community and extoll the ability to draw near to the Divine as a sacred gift. Notice here that this practice of atonement does not happen in a vacuum. The community always deals with sins communally and with the help of the priests to make sure the sacrifices do not accidentally become profane. This priestly action is echoed in the current form of confession: In the modern rite of reconciliation, the priest stands in for the whole community of the church in announcing the pardon gifted by God to us.

> In the modern rite of reconciliation, the priest stands in for the whole community of the church in announcing the pardon gifted by God to us.

The Bible tells of other penitential practices: supplication, fasting, mourning, wearing sackcloth—all ways people have tried to deal with the damage caused by sin. But these actions can never fully take away the influence of cosmic Sin. To heal the relationship, God decided to intervene on our behalf. So God sent Jesus, the Paschal Lamb, to be the full and perfect sacrifice for our sins—and not for our sins only but for the sins of the whole world. In Christian theology, the view of Jesus as the Paschal Lamb draws on the sacrificial rituals of the Hebrews. Again, these sacrifices are seen as atoning actions to bring humans and God closer after having been in sinful discord. By virtue of his fully human and fully divine nature, Jesus is the ultimate sacrifice because he brings the realm of God and humans together in a way that cannot be separated.

We see this view of Jesus throughout the New Testament. Scholar Ian Bradly writes,

> John's Gospel introduces a…ritualistic element of sacrifice into the treatment of Jesus' death as, for example, in the reference to the flow of blood and water from his side. This aspect is more emphatically emphasized in other books in the New Testament, notably in the Epistle to the Hebrews which clearly locates Jesus' death in the context of the Israelite cult and presents him as the ultimate high priest who, through shedding his own blood, has made a perfect and all-sufficient atonement for the sins of the world… The book of Revelation in its dramatic portrayal of the lamb slain from the foundation of the world highlights a motif found elsewhere in the New Testament where sacrifice is presented as revelatory of the eternal and essential character of God.[5]

In other words, Jesus tells us in the Gospel of John that God did not send his son into the world to condemn the world, but to save the world through him (3:17). And because of that gift, there are now no unforgivable sins. Even for those guilty of "serious" sins, God will deny love to no one and has already extended joyful forgiveness to the one who repents. God's unique position as the Paschal Lamb who is also the High Priest means that God alone can declare such eternal and permanent pardon. And just like that, we no longer need any sacrifice for the atonement of our sin. God has already fulfilled that in Christ.

Of course, even after Jesus' life and death and resurrection, people kept sinning. And this became a problem for the early church. How could they be faithful followers of Jesus—and still sin right and left? The Rite of Reconciliation developed in response to this reality—in our humanness we are prone to sin. But the rite also reflects the New Testament understanding of all-encompassing forgiveness offered to those who are repentant. Guided by Jesus' words of binding and loosening of sins in Matthew 16:19 and 18:18 as well as the forgiving and retaining of sins in John 20:23, the early church sought a way to help people reconcile with God.

Over the past 2,000 years, confession has been practiced in many forms, from public displays of punishment to purchasing indulgences to our modern rite. Yet throughout history, different communities have sought an answer to essentially the same question: How can we, who have been forgiven, be able to live without sinning? The answer is to follow Jesus—he forgave and so must we—and that includes forgiving ourselves. Sin is never the final answer of who we are or whose we are. The church—the Body of Christ—gives us the pastoral tool of Reconciliation of a Penitent to live as though sin has no power over us. The bad news is that we will sin, likely again and again. But the good news has been, is, and always will be that we are never alone in our sin. We always have the offer of God to be united with God, and in Jesus, we see that invitation and reality in its fullest form.

# History of Confession

The concept of confession in the church has changed over time. In the first centuries after Jesus' death and resurrection, penitence often included rigorous public displays of punishment for those guilty of great sins. Episcopal Bishop Neil Alexander explores this changing nature of confession, writing,

> The penitents wore goatskin clothing (the hide of the damned), were refused bathing privileges, were required to keep strict fasts, and were to undergo an almost endless process of physical and spiritual mortification. On Sundays, the penitents were present only for the Liturgy of the Word and its moral exhortations [and were made to kneel in service] instead of enjoying the customary posture of the resurrection, standing.[6]

Perhaps the worst part of this treatment was a ban against partaking in communion until Easter morning. Since receiving Holy Eucharist meant that you were part of the one Body of Christ, it was deemed improper to have a notorious sinner "contaminate" the whole Christian group. It will probably not surprise you to find out that these extreme practices did not last forever!

As early as the seventh century, the rite changed from a public confession to a private one and from being practiced once or twice in a lifetime to yearly, then weekly, and even more frequently. Instead of public humiliation and a prolonged season of living as a penitent, people were called to privately confess to their priest and to receive absolution from the church alone. As confession moved into a private interaction between priest and penitent, "more private forms of reconciliation developed based on an increasingly elaborate system of penitential 'tariffs' imposed upon the penitents as the cost of their absolution. Such tariffs were penitential acts assigned according to the severity of the sin."[7] Celtic Christian traditions in particular brought about the spread of *penitentials* (essentially formulas to calculate the proper penance for a sin). For example, one source notes that, "If some woman by her magic misleads a woman with respect to the birth of a child, she shall do penance for half a year with an allowance of bread and water and abstain for two years from wine and meats and fast for six forty-day periods with bread and water."[8] As you may remember from your high school history or religion class,

this system led to abuse by some clergy who began to use the act of penitence, such as charging for indulgences for personal gain.

During the Reformation, the onset of Protestant denominations changed confession again. Reformers tended to underplay or do away entirely with private confession in response to abuses in the Roman Catholic tradition and the selling of indulgences. Instead the emerging Protestant traditions favored general corporate confession. Although the Reformers did not completely eliminate confession, they made considerable changes in the practice.[9]

These changes were felt in England where the Anglican Church's reform efforts were spearheaded by Thomas Cranmer, archbishop of Canterbury. Cranmer, known as the architect of the first *Book of Common Prayer*, did not include a special rite of reconciliation in the first edition, printed in 1549. There was provision for confession during visitation of the sick, but people were encouraged to seek out reconciliation chiefly in private prayer and during corporate worship.[10] Indeed, this approach to reconciliation personifies what we now call the Anglican "middle way," drawing upon both Lutheran and Reformed practices and doctrines.

In the nineteenth century, proponents of the Oxford Movement revisited the concept of a Rite of Reconciliation. Members of this liturgical movement were interested in reviving many pre-Reformation practices within the Anglican Church. Alongside the Oxford movement was the revival of religious orders of both women and men, which helped to make confession a more widely used aspect of Christian discipleship.

This desire to reclaim a rite of reconciliation spread to America. In addition to the liturgical renewal championed by the Oxford Movement, there was a growing understanding of the therapeutic value of talking about problems and sins. Coupled with the growth of a "more ecumenical climate, confession ceased to be automatically under suspicion as a practice associated with Roman Catholicism and could be judged on its own merits."[11] This change led to the inclusion of two options (forms) for the Rite of Reconciliation of a Penitent in the 1979 revision (and current edition) of *The Book of Common Prayer*. Reconciliation of a Penitent has been a part of our tradition ever since.

# Response

One of the gifts of history (both individual and corporate history) is the ability to look back over time for signs of God's presence moving in our lives. It is also important to be honest about when we have chosen our own sinful desires over God's call. Life with God can be thought of as walking a path with many twists and turns, dead-ends, and wide-open stretches. The need for reconciliation comes especially at those times we have veered off the path from our true selves. When we are reconciled, we turn around and move back in the direction that God would have us go.

In a journal, the worksheet in the Appendix (page 131), or other place of reflection, spend some time writing about key decisions that you have made in your life. Include important relationships, school choices, vocational choices, major illnesses, etc. It might be helpful to use different colors to represent different emotions or values that helped inform your decisions at each moment. Be as honest as you can with both your joys and disappointments, when your decisions seemed to align with God's call and when they didn't. Using these events and feelings as plot points, draw a line that represents the path that you have walked in your life. Where have you walked on God's path and where have you followed your own? What happened during those times? Where might God lead you in the future?

If you are in a group setting—and if you feel comfortable— share your reflections and listen to others' responses.

# Reflection

Following God's path requires identifying our core values. These are the principles that guide our choices, sometimes without us even being aware of them. Use the questions below to help identify your core values.

If you are in a group setting—and if you feel comfortable—share your reflections and listen to others' responses.

+ How would you describe yourself?

+ How would you describe your relationship with God? With your closest friend or loved one? With the person who troubles your spirit the most?

+ What three moments, places, people, or things have helped you feel most alive in your life?

+ What do you hope your legacy will be?

+ What values were you taught as a child?

+ What values do you think are important to teach a child?

+ What are three values that you hope to live by? Do you? Why or why not?

# Closing

In this prayer time, feel free to let your creative side help you find healing and comfort with this activity designed to help you name and release your sin. Naming your sins can have the effect of taking away some of their burden and weight since we often feel the most shame about the things we find most unspeakable. Choose one of these three activities to begin to name and let go of sins in your life:

- ✛ Using a washable marker, write any sin you need to name on a coffee filter or dissolvable paper and place it in a bowl of water. The paper will dissolve or the ink will blend together, reminding us of the healing nature of our baptism to remove all our sins.

- ✛ Taking a shallow container full of sand, write everything you would like to confess with your fingertip and then gently wipe it away with your palm. This sand recalls the time the Israelites spent in the wilderness when God released them from their bondage.

- ✛ Calling to mind the great new fire of hope that we light every year at the Easter Vigil, write your sins on a piece of paper (page 132) and then (safely) burn them.

## Prayer

Holy One, you are the source of all holy and humble things. Help me to strip away the things that clutter my vision of you and turn my heart to the direction of your simplicity. Give me courage in place of fear, love instead of indifference, and life in the face of death. Let me place those things that break down the peace you offer into your hands and grant me the strength to release them. Be with me as I follow your path that leads to all light and love. I ask this in the name of the one God: Creator, Redeemer, and Sustainer. **Amen.**

# 3

# Shame, Guilt, and Joy

*Then the father said to him, "Son, you are always with me, and all that is mine is yours. But we had to celebrate and rejoice, because this brother of yours was dead and has come to life; he was lost and has been found."*

—Luke 15:31-32

*Create in me a clean heart, O God.*

—Psalm 51:11

# Opening Prayer

Almighty God, you know that we have no power in ourselves to help ourselves: Keep us both outwardly in our bodies and inwardly in our souls, that we may be defended from all adversities which may happen to the body, and from all evil thoughts which may assault and hurt the soul; through Jesus Christ our Lord, who lives and reigns with you and the Holy Spirit, one God, for ever and ever. **Amen.**

—*THE BOOK OF COMMON PRAYER, P. 218*

# The Difference between Shame and Guilt

As we explored in previous chapters, part of our human history is wrapped up in the way we deal with our sin and the way it has put us in wrong relationship with God, others, and ourselves. Biblically, theologically, and liturgically, we know that Jesus offers us the opportunity to live differently and to be reconciled back to God through him. Yet in our modern times, psychotherapy has become the tool of choice for many to deal with shame and guilt that can arise from our sinful actions. We have become very sophisticated in dealing with sin—or so we may be tempted to think.

In truth, there is still a need to look at our own actions in a healthy way and to investigate our own responsibility for our actions. Ironically, in doing so and confessing to God, we are invited to live free from the pain and suffering that these feelings cause and to live in joy. We actually get to let go of that baggage that we carry around with us! To understand this great joy, let's take a closer look at the baggage in the first place— the experience of shame and guilt.

The science of psychology has given us the gift of a deeper understanding of the emotions of guilt and shame and the control that they can have over our lives. This is very helpful since these emotions are both very powerful and often easily confused. As sociologist Robert Karen puts it, "The same experience can arouse both guilt and shame, or guilt in one person and shame in another, based on their psychological and cultural makeup." Karen writes that the important distinction between the two is that "guilt is about transgression and shame is about self. Guilt is about behavior that has harmed others; shame is about not being 'good enough.' To be ashamed is to expect rejection, not so much because of what one has done as because of what one is."[12] In other words, guilt means that you have made a true mistake, and your actions have wronged someone or something. Shame, on the other hand, makes you feel that you are a mistake, and therefore worthless.

> Guilt means that you have made a true mistake, and your actions have wronged someone or something. Shame, on the other hand, makes you feel that you are a mistake, and therefore worthless.

Guilt is not a bad thing for us to feel in healthy amounts. It can help us acknowledge the sins we have committed against God, others, and ourselves and take responsibility for them. Using the same example from the Introduction, if you yelled at your kids unwarrantedly, you might say to yourself, "I got angry and yelled at my kids. I was tired but that doesn't make it right. I made a mistake. I need to apologize." Indeed, only sociopaths do not feel guilt for their actions, believing that they are above all condemnation.

However, shame can make us feel worthless and is rooted in the way we perceive ourselves. Using the same example, if you yelled at your kids but internalized shame about yourself, then your inner dialogue might sound like this: "I got angry and yelled at my kids because I am a terrible parent. I never should have had kids. I'll probably end up messing them up too." With this kind of unhealthy mindset, it becomes impossible to believe that you can be forgiven or that you could deserve forgiveness. You stop believing that you can ever change.

Often, guilt and shame take on negative pathological dimensions and become destructive. There is evidence that when a person holds onto guilt and shame, they are affected in physiological ways, impacting bodily health as well as the mind and spirit. But we don't need scientific data to prove this—all you have to do is think of a time when you were ashamed or embarrassed and remember the way your stomach tied up in knots or your face flushed with heat. We don't just experience guilt or shame—we end up wearing it. When we can purge ourselves of this guilt and shame with God's help, we are able to lay these emotions down and live as new creations, free from these burdens. The Rite of Reconciliation of a Penitent gives us the space to speak about these things in a place of love and healing. This action of reconciliation can lead to joy.

Many people seek therapy to deal with their feelings of guilt and shame. I am a big supporter and recipient of therapy, and I believe it can be a useful tool in exploring these truths and emotions. But therapy should not be a replacement for the Rite of Reconciliation (and conversely, in many situations, people who have experienced the Rite of Reconciliation would benefit from therapy as well). With the prevalence of counselors and psychologists, we have become deft at "talking out" feelings of shame (that may be confused with guilt) and finding relief in the good work that can occur in therapy. This move toward health is a wonderful thing, but it misses the most important gift: the kind of healing that comes only from God. Therapy doesn't offer forgiveness. Only God does that.

God knows us in every way and yet still loves us. Recall the story of the Prodigal Son (Luke 15:11-32) or the passage from 1 John 3:19-20: "And by this we will know that we are

> Therapy should not be a replacement for the Rite of Reconciliation.

from the truth and will reassure our hearts before him whenever our hearts condemn us; for God is greater than our hearts, and he knows everything." God knows our guilt and shame and still offers us forgiveness and new life. God's grace trumps shame because who you are will always be loved by God who made you and not by error. God's grace trumps guilt because Jesus has taken all our sins unto himself and set us free from that pain. While therapy can offer us a way to deal with the pain of guilt and shame, only God's grace experienced in the reconciling action of Christ can offer us full healing and new life.

# Response

Feelings of guilt and shame can be felt in the body as well as the soul. In this meditation, we will use an art therapy technique to enrich our prayers. Using the illustration below or the worksheet in the Appendix (page 133), divide the heart into sections that represent things that you would like for God to heal. Perhaps there are things that you are feeling legitimately guilty about, or maybe there are things for which you feel shame. Perhaps there are areas of brokenness caused by your own wrongdoings or ways in which you have been harmed. Feel free to use many different colors and shapes to create the heart that you would like to offer to God for healing and wholeness.

Say this prayer as you finish: "Create in me a clean heart, O God."

If you are in a group setting—and if you feel comfortable— share your reflections and listen to others' responses.

# Reflection

In the blank calendar below or on a full-size one in the Appendix (page 134), draw or write a symbol or word for the healing grace that you have seen in your life today instead of shame.

For example, if you had a conversation with someone that included forgiveness, record that here. Or if you saw something in nature, like a sunrise, that reminded you of the wide love of God, write that down as well.

| SUNDAY | MONDAY | TUESDAY | WEDNESDAY |
|--------|--------|---------|-----------|
|        |        |         |           |

| THURSDAY | FRIDAY | SATURDAY |
|----------|--------|----------|
|          |        |          |

# Closing

Today's prayer is taken from *Praying with the Body* by Roy DeLeon.[13] Since guilt and shame physically manifest in our lives, let us join in this time of prayer to ask God to free us from this burden—mind, body, and soul. These body prayers can be done alone or in a group.

*If reading as a group, the bold indicates the group response.*

*Illustrations of ways for the body to join in prayer can be found in the Appendix, page 135.*

## Opening Prayer

Into your hands, O Lord, I commit my spirit.
> **Glory to you, Creator, Redeemer, Sanctifier.**
> **Now and Forever. Amen.**

## Reading

Have mercy on me, O God,
> **according to your steadfast love;**

according to your abundant mercy
> **blot out my transgressions.**

Against you, you alone, have I sinned,
> **and done what is evil in your sight,**

so that you are justified in your sentence
> **and blameless when you pass judgment.**

You desire truth in the inward being;
> **therefore teach me wisdom in my secret heart.**

Create in me a clean heart, O God,
> **and put a new and right spirit within me.**

O Lord, open my lips,
> **and my mouth will declare your praise.**

For you have no delight in sacrifice;
> **if I were to give a burnt-offering, you would not be pleased.**

The sacrifice acceptable to God is a broken spirit;
> **a broken and contrite heart, O God, you will not despise.**

—Selections from Psalm 51 (NRSV)

## Reflection

✣ How does being forgiven for your mistakes or offenses make you feel?

✣ How does forgiveness feel in your heart, in your energy level, in the way you carry yourself?

✣ How can you ask God to purify your heart of all shame and guilt?

*A moment of silence may be offered.*

## Praying with the Body, Heart, And Soul

**Hear me, O Merciful One.**
*Inhale: Quietly express your prayer with your body, heart, and soul*

**Clear my conscience in your love.**
*Exhale: Breathe out guilt, regrets, shame, and blame.*

**Your truth permeates my whole being.**
*Inhale: With an open heart, inhale God's truth.*

**Your wisdom fills my heart.**
*Exhale: Bowing down, thank God for the wisdom to know love from fear.*

*Joy in Confession*

**Fill me with your loving Spirit;**
> *Inhale: Be inspired, renewed, and revitalized as you inhale.*

**Cleanse my heart of wrath, greed, and gluttony.**
> *Exhale: Feel lightened, emptied, and open for God's love.*

**Rid my lips of lies and deceit, O God.**
> *Inhale: Lift your chin, soften your lips, open your mouth to receive goodness, truth and beauty.*

**Let them instead declare your love.**
> *Exhale: Bow your head to the love that never fails.*

**Accept and heal my broken spirit;**
> *Inhale: Look up and offer your soul for comfort and healing.*

**Teach me to be humble of heart.**
> *Exhale: Be the child of God that you are: loved, loving, and lovable..*

## Sitting with the Divine Presence

Sitting in silence, mindfully observe your breathing in and breathing out. Stay aware of the Divine Presence. Now visualize your heart as God's garden. Spring has come, and it's time to attend to the garden. See the Gardener with a wide hat, long sleeves, and gloves. Hear the Gardner talk to blossoms coming forth from bulbs and seeds long ago planted and sown. But with the blooming plants, some weeds come up also. So the Gardner bends down and patiently pulls each weed and anything harmful from the garden of your heart. As you sit and breathe, witness and allow the cleansing actions of God in your heart. Give thanks to the Gardener.

## Silent Prayer

*A moment of silence may be offered.*

## Contemporary Psalm

*May be said in unison or by the leader.*

O most compassionate Heart,

Forgive my faults and offense,

Forgive my misguided trips into darkness.
Puffed up by pride and vanity,

I declined your life-giving counsel.

Teach me obedience and humility, Oh God,
Help me see and change my unkind ways.

Cleanse my heart and restore my soul. A wounded spirit
and a broken heart—That's all I can offer you, my God.

## Closing Prayer

Bring your palms flat onto your chest. Then looking up with soft eyes, say, "Lord, please heal me, if you wish. Forgiveness and healing come only from you." **Amen.**

# 4

# Kenosis, Forgiveness, and Release

*Let the same mind be in you that was in Christ Jesus, who, though he was in the form of God, did not regard equality with God as something to be exploited, but emptied himself, taking the form of a slave, being born in human likeness. And being found in human form, he humbled himself and became obedient to the point of death— even death on a cross. Therefore God also highly exalted him and gave him the name that is above every name, so that at the name of Jesus every knee should bend, in heaven and on earth and under the earth, and every tongue should confess that Jesus Christ is Lord, to the glory of God the Father.*

-Philippians 2:5-11

# Opening Prayers

O God, who for our redemption gave your only-begotten Son to the death of the cross, and by his glorious resurrection delivered us from the power of our enemy; Grant us so to die daily to sin, that we may evermore live with him in the joy of his resurrection; through Jesus Christ your Son our Lord, who lives and reigns with you and the Holy Spirit, one God, now and forever. **Amen.**

—*The Book of Common Prayer*, p. 222

# Kenosis as a Biblical Concept

We have been exploring the delicate balance between sin and reconciliation. This chapter helps us understand how to leave brokenness behind by following Jesus' expression of true humility and the concept of *kenosis*.

The term kenosis means emptying; it is derived from a Greek word found in Paul's letter to the Philippians: "Christ Jesus… emptied himself, taking the form of a slave, being born in human likeness" (The full passage is printed at the opening of this chapter). There has been much debate about what Paul is trying to say about the nature of Jesus when he took on human form. For our purposes, however, we will view this mystery as an example of Jesus' extreme humility: Even though he is Lord and King, Jesus was willing to put aside any pride of station and live and die as one of us and bear our sins. We too should empty ourselves of our pride and strive to be like Jesus.

Anglican theologian A.M. Allchin notes, "The passage [in Philippians] speaks of the humility and obedience of Christ, not in terms of incidents taken from the course of his life, or of speculations about his psychological motivation. What we have is an affirmation of more than temporal and local import. Christ freely and willingly exchanges equality with God for the form of a slave. He moves from the divine realm to the human, from the world of eternity, to the world of time, making himself open and vulnerable to death, death on the cross."[14]

The call to kenosis—to an emptying of self—is hard for us to embrace. To paraphrase the great theologian Karl Barth, humanity's chief sin is always pride. We always try to put ourselves in control, in God's place. We experience this every time we choose greed instead of choosing to live simply—or when we live outside our means, not being grateful for what we already have.

> We humans are created in God's likeness and are called to empty ourselves on behalf of God. This emptying—kenosis—helps us to love fully as God does.

Yet, in Christ we see that God's way is to choose humility. The true joy and mystery about Jesus' incarnation is that he transcends himself, as Allchin writes, "in order to enter into his own creation, and in doing so, opens the possibility for his human creation to transcend itself, to go beyond itself, in a responsive movement of total self-giving."[15] In other words, because Jesus came to us as both fully human and fully divine, he shows us the true measure of humanity—that we humans are created in God's likeness and are called to empty ourselves on behalf of God. This emptying—kenosis—helps us to love fully as God does.

This humility is not a self-debasement but a self-forgetting and setting aside the false side. It is an ability to lay aside your ego and view yourself as God sees you—as a beloved child who has been baptized and is now one with Jesus Christ. This is a gift of grace that will let you begin to see how God dwells within you.

Reconciliation of a Penitent offers us a way to practice this Christ-like kenosis. When we humble ourselves and confess our sins and ask God to empty us of all our brokenness and pride, we are reminded of our true identity and can be filled with the Holy Spirit.

# Response

The grace of kenosis is that it lets us empty ourselves of pride and sin so that we can be filled with the Holy Spirit. Imagine a bowl filled to the brim with heavy rocks. If you tried to pour water in that bowl, there would only be space for a little water between and around the stones. But if you emptied that bowl, how much life-giving water could be added?

Imagine in this same bowl a mirror on the bottom that lets you see yourself as God truly sees you—a beloved child. You can still see that image when the bowl is filled with the Living Water of the Holy Spirit. But when it's filled with distractions and sins, the image is distorted and blocked.

To carry out this exercise, you can either use the drawing of a bowl in the Appendix (page 136), or an actual one (perhaps a heavy paper or plastic bowl). Decorate it using markers or pencils. On the bottom of your bowl, draw an icon or a symbol of how you envision your true essence as a child of God. For example, you might draw a cross or butterfly or a self-portrait—anything that represents your true self. Next, write down on strips of paper or on the drawing things that are separating you from seeing your self. You might return to the first chapter for some reminders.

If using a real bowl, place the strips of paper in a bowl. These are the things that need to be reconciled back to God. These are the things that need to be laid before God so that we might experience the grace of Christ-like kenosis.

Holding your hand over the bowl (or the paper), say a prayer, asking God for the strength and courage to empty yourself of these distractions. Then discard the paper/strips as a symbol of new beginning.

# Reflection

We continue to reflect upon our lives, looking for the identity that God calls us to as well as the grace that God offers us. One tool in this journey is to engage in the classic practice of the Daily Examine from St. Ignatius of Loyola. This technique calls us to daily reflection on a day's events, to rummage through our days and see where God's presence was seen and where we responded (or should have) to God's grace and love. Using the form below, pick a time of your day (traditionally at noon or in the evening) to conduct your own Daily Examine. While you are in prayer, look for God's grace and invitation to kenosis, opportunities to empty yourself of those things that stop you from fully embracing God.

1. Become aware of God's presence.
2. Review the day with gratitude.
3. Pay attention to your emotions.
4. Choose one feature of the day and pray about it.
5. Look toward tomorrow.

# Closing

Today's prayer time is adapted from *Living in the Green*, a program written by Courtney V. Cowart and James M. Goodmann and offered by the Beecken Center of the School of Theology at the University of the South. *Living in the Green* offers tools for church leaders who want to renew and deepen their spiritual lives.[16]

Since kenosis is about emptying ourselves of our pride and following Jesus' example, our meditation will help us begin to let God open our hearts and hands. A guide from *Living in the Green* notes, "With a human nature that is often resistant to change, there is yet another discipline we need to practice—Letting Go. Letting go of old habits of the heart, mind, and will is necessary before we are really ready to let new ideas and inspirations fill us and move us into the future. This practice helps us to empty our 'old wine skins' and make room for the 'new wine.'

"Letting Go is an opportunity to suspend patterned ways of knowing that may be 'stuck,' or that serve as a crutch that we no longer need. Letting Go is aimed at our tendency to exercise sole control over our lives [which is a mark of pride]. This exercise is an invitation to the renewing work of the Holy Spirit, which holds our lives, both the good and the bad, and offers transformation and reconciliation."

# Reading

Let the same mind be in you that was in Christ Jesus, who, though he was in the form of God, did not regard equality with God as something to be exploited, but emptied himself, taking the form of a slave, being born in human likeness. And being found in human form, he humbled himself and became obedient to the point of death—even death on a cross.

Therefore God also highly exalted him and gave him the name that is above every name, so that at the name of Jesus every knee should bend, in heaven and on earth and under the earth, and every tongue should confess that Jesus Christ is Lord, to the glory of God the Father.

—PHILIPPIANS 2:5-11

## Praying with the Body, Heart, And Soul

- ✝ Begin by asking God to enter into your body, heart, and soul.

- ✝ Sit in a chair and take a moment to center yourself. Take a few deep breaths, in and out. Get yourself ready to be present to this moment.

- ✝ Close your eyes.

- ✝ Find a place on your seat that you can grip with your hands. Imagine that there is zero gravity in the room and the only way you can stay in your chair is to hold onto it for dear life. Imagine that if you let go you would float away.

- ✝ Don't stop holding the chair. With your eyes still closed, summon a negative belief you have about yourself or something you are ashamed of. Squeezing your chair more tightly, imagine that you are holding on to this negative belief. Hold it tightly for eight seconds—as if your very life depended on it.

- ✝ Now, release your grip on the chair, and as you do so, also release this negative belief. Experience the belief floating away, up away from your body, over your head, through the ceiling, and into the sky. Let it go. Untether it. Feel yourself being untied from it.

- ✛ Now, imagine a positive belief about yourself or something you are really proud of.

- ✛ Grip the chair tightly again and hold onto this positive belief. Hold tightly to it for eight seconds.

- ✛ Now release the chair and the belief. Unhand them. Just let them go.

- ✛ Sit in silence, mindfully observing your breathing in and breathing out. Ask God to fill you up with the Holy Spirit.

## Closing Prayer

Gracious and loving God, we know that you carry us as though on eagles' wings and bring us to ourselves. Keep us ever awake to the knowledge that you are the very air we breathe and the source of our freedom. Let that knowledge echo in our hearts so that we may believe that we have been created for greater things than we can ever ask or imagine, if we but release our cares to you. May our spirits take flight, sure in the joy that you are our God. **Amen.**

# 5

# Resurrection
# and Incarnation

*At an acceptable time I have listened to you, and on a day of salvation I have helped you. See, now is the acceptable time; see, now is the day of salvation!*

—2 Corinthians 6:2

# Opening Prayer

Almighty and everlasting God, who in the Paschal mystery established the new covenant of reconciliation: Grant that all who have been reborn into the fellowship of Christ's Body may show forth in their lives what they profess by their faith; through Jesus Christ our Lord, who lives and reigns with you and the Holy Spirit, one God, for ever and ever. **Amen.**

—*THE BOOK OF COMMON PRAYER*, p. 223

# Living as a New Creation

Congratulations! You have made it to the best chapter. Actually, it's even better than simply making it to a certain part of a book—you have made it to the best part of life with Christ: resurrected living! During the previous chapters, we have delved deeper into the call of reconciliation that God extends to us. We have looked at the history of sin and confession, examined the difference between guilt and shame, and spent some time following Jesus' example of kenosis. This chapter marks a shift for us as we move past the broken parts of our lives and relationships into the new creation that Paul talks about in his second letter to the Corinthians. This shift can be as dramatic as turning from the dark desert feeling of Lent to the "Alleluia! Christ is risen!" joy of Easter! It is life-changing—in fact, it is new-life making!

So let's explore what it means to live as a new creation. As we have discussed, sin is corrosive to the soul because it corrupts our relationships with ourselves, others, and God. We have seen how sin works to lead us away from our true identities as children of God who have joined Christ in his death and resurrection. As Christians, we believe this union with Jesus—his sacrifice and rise to glory—is central to what it means to be a part of the Body of Christ here on earth. We believe this is so important that we claim baptism—the rite in which we join in Christ's death through the baptismal waters and then emerge from this watery grave having "put on Christ"—as the initiation into the faith. In *The Book of Common Prayer* (pages 306-307), we hear these powerful tones of rebirth and transformation in the prayers of thanksgiving over the water that invoke the whole story of God's movement in creation. We hear how the Holy Spirit moved over the waters of creation, how the Israelites were led to freedom out of bondage through the Red Sea, and how Jesus himself was baptized in the waters of the Jordan River. This pattern of creation, salvation, and transformation is exactly what we are invited to recall and experience through baptism. The Holy Spirit moves over the waters of our lives and calls us to freedom from the sins that enslave us. And when we rise out of the waters, we are transformed, joining with Jesus and living as a part of his Body—the Church.

> The Holy Spirit moves over the waters of our lives and calls us to freedom from the sins that enslave us.

Baptism is no small thing! It is not, for example, enough to simply claim allegiance with Jesus' ideals to be considered a Christian. One has to be baptized first as a mark of entering into his Body, the Church. Paul highlights this baptismal imperative when he writes,

> Do you not know that all of us who have been baptized into Christ Jesus were baptized into his death? Therefore we have been buried with him by baptism into death, so that, just as Christ was raised from the dead by the glory of the Father, so we too might walk in newness of life. For if we have been united with him in a death like his, we will certainly be united with him in a resurrection like his. We know that our old self was crucified with him so that the body of sin might be destroyed, and we might no longer be enslaved to sin.
>
> —ROMANS 6:3-6

In other words, in this new life with Christ that is opened to us at our baptism, we find that our old self (the self that was weighed down by sin) has been made a new creation. We are slaves of sin and death no more.

How does this resurrection work in our life? The amazing reality about the baptismal life Paul describes is that it makes resurrection a possibility for us—not just in the afterlife, but in this realm as well. Resurrection then does not just refer to the major resurrection of Jesus to eternal life. Through reconciliation, our whole lives become series of small deaths and resurrections that are touched by the grace of God. We die to sin repeatedly and are raised to the new life of grace repeatedly. Reconciliation of a Penitent is an important tool in this pattern of new living. We are called, as Paul says in his second letter to the Corinthians, to live as new creations now— today—as well as in the future because we have been saved from the death of sin. He writes:

> Through reconciliation, our whole lives become series of small deaths and resurrections that are touched by the grace of God.

> So if anyone is in Christ, there is a new creation: everything old has passed away; see, everything has become new! All this is from God, who reconciled us to himself through Christ, and has given us the ministry of reconciliation; that is, in Christ God was reconciling the world to himself, not counting their trespasses against them, and entrusting the message of reconciliation to us. So we are ambassadors for Christ, since God is making his appeal through us; we entreat you on behalf of Christ, be reconciled to God. For our sake he made him to be sin who knew no sin, so that in him we might become the righteousness of God. As we work together with him, we urge you also not to accept the grace of God in vain. For he says, "At an acceptable time I have listened to you, and on a day of salvation I have helped you." See, now is the acceptable time; see, now is the day of salvation!
>
> —2 CORINTHIANS 5:17—6:2

Paul is reminding us that we should not keep sinning as though we have not been resurrected from that deadly way of life. Since we have been baptized, we must now see these days as the days of salvation. When we sin, we are given the grace to be reconciled to Christ again through the Rite of Reconciliation, which God has graced us with and calls us to bring to the world as his "ambassadors of reconciliation." The other beautiful part of this transformation is how joyful Paul's tone is in this passage. We have been made into something new. And this is something to be excited about! Our joy cannot—should not—be contained, and we are motivated—as the Church and as individuals—to change the world into that joy-filled place. It's no wonder that one of the most beloved images of Easter is the butterfly. Born to spread its wings and soar, the butterfly is bound until it is transformed from the chrysalis. When we emerge from the tombs or the chrysalis that we have been held in, we live as we were truly designed to—and our lives will never be the same. Thanks be to God!

# Response

In this meditation, we join with all the ordinary people who have heard the voice of God and been called to do extraordinary things. In the cycle of reconciliation, we ask God to create a space in us by letting go of the burdens of sin we carry. The meditation from the last chapter was a way of practicing this kenosis or letting go. As we know from scripture, Christ frees us from our burdens so that we might be filled with new life and live as a new creation in the world, bringing others to his love. When we are reconciled back to God, we are given our vocation and our future life's shape. Thus, we will spend some time in prayer and discernment by taking a mental journey into the future.

Gather six to ten stones and a permanent marker—or use the paper with illustrated stones found in the Appendix on page 137. Spend 5-10 minutes in silence. Clear your mind of your own wants and needs, your to-do lists and demands, and listen. Try to hear what God is saying to you. (You might follow the instructions from last week for praying with the body, heart, and soul.) After your silence is over, write on the first stone where you are now, and on the last, where God wants you to be. This can be in your personal life, spiritual life, or professional life—or all three! Now fill in the stones with incremental steps that can help you move into the future God is calling you to.

If you are in a group setting—and if you feel comfortable—share your reflections and listen to others' responses.

# Reflection

Now that you have identified the path toward new life, create an icon of the vision of the future God has given you. An icon does not need to be a perfect picture of the face of Jesus or a saint—indeed traditional icons are never meant to be this. An icon can be a representation of a spiritual truth. Consider it a window on our resurrected life. An icon can be a representation of a heavenly vision in whatever form you like. Jot down phrases or ideas, or draw or paint a version of the future that you saw. A worksheet is available in the Resources section of the Appendix (page 138). This icon will be a guiding tool as we seek to become the ambassadors of Christ that we are called to be.

# Closing

Today's liturgy is adapted from *Living in the Green*. The exercise is intended to slow us down long enough for an encounter with God. It supports envisioning a glimpse of the future within us that is waiting to emerge, an echo of Luke's Gospel that the "Kingdom of God is within you" (17:21).

"Throughout the Christian story, we find ordinary people who have done extraordinary things because of their encounter with the Holy. We cannot enact what we have not first seen within us and among us. When we engage this meditation, we become more aware of the presence of God and more conscious of the deeper longings within us.

"While we worship, we will be asking God to open our hearts to the future that God is calling us to. With the help of the Holy Spirit, we will be discerning the new creation that we are called to through our baptisms. As we meditate on our lives with God, let us rejoice that we have joined with Jesus in his resurrection." [17]

## Reading

So if anyone is in Christ, there is a new creation: everything old has passed away; see, everything has become new! All this is from God, who reconciled us to himself through Christ, and has given us the ministry of reconciliation; that is, in Christ God was reconciling the world to himself, not counting their trespasses against them, and entrusting the message of reconciliation to us. So we are ambassadors for Christ, since God is making his appeal through us; we entreat you on behalf of Christ, be reconciled to God. For our sake he made him to be sin who knew no sin, so that in him we might become the righteousness of God. As we work together with him, we urge you also not to accept the grace of God in vain. For he says,

"At an acceptable time I have listened to you, and on a day of salvation I have helped you." See, now is the acceptable time; see, now is the day of salvation!

—2 Corinthians 5:17—6:2

## Praying with the Body, Heart, and Soul

Let us ask God to enter into our body, mind, and soul.

✛ Find a comfortable place and position. Close your eyes.

✛ Take a few deep breaths. Release. Repeat until you feel peaceful and at rest.

✛ Free your mind of your worry, concerns, questions, excitement, or enthusiasm. Open your mind, heart, and will.

✛ Now journey down from your head into your heart. Try to become in tune with your feelings and surroundings.

✛ Imagine standing at a doorway of a possible future where you are caring for your relationships between yourself, others, and God. Imagine a future where you are responding to a call to be an ambassador for reconciliation.

✛ Take one step forward. What do you see past that doorway into the future?

✛ Step through the threshold of the doorway into the future.

✛ Turn around 360 degrees. What do you see? What's different? Who is there? What is the mood? How are you feeling? What are the sounds?

✛ From that future place, look back through the doorway to the past and find yourself. What advice do you give your past self to move forward to the future self you see?

✢ Walk back through the doorway and return again to the present. Write what you saw, felt, and heard. Be as specific as you can about the images, feelings, and activities that took place in your vision.

✢ Using the response above, revisit the icon that you created. Do you need to add anything to the icon? Take away something? Continue to make revisions based on your prayers and discernment.

## Closing Prayer

O changeless and merciful God, we know that you are at work changing the parts of us that need to be healed, smoothed, or perfected. Help us to trust in our work, even if it is slow. Help us to listen to your invitation to change, even when you call to us with a still, small voice. Help us to believe in your power, even when we fail to see it at work in the world around us. Help us to give our whole life to you so that we would become the people you created us to be. **Amen.**

# 6

# Growth from Forgiveness

*And Jesus came and said to them, "All authority in heaven and on earth has been given to me. Go therefore and make disciples of all nations, baptizing them in the name of the Father and of the Son and of the Holy Spirit, and teaching them to obey everything that I have commanded you. And remember, I am with you always, to the end of the age."*

—Matthew 28:18-20

# Opening Prayer

*O God, whose Son Jesus is the good shepherd of your people: Grant that when we hear his voice we may know him who calls us each by name, and follow where he leads; who, with you and the Holy Spirit, lives and reigns, one God, for ever and ever.* **Amen.**

—*THE BOOK OF COMMON PRAYER*, p. 225

# The Great Commission

Throughout this book, we have reflected and participated in the arc of reconciliation. We have learned about the way sin has affected all of humanity and about our place in salvation history. We have explored the balance between guilt and shame. We have practiced Christ-centered kenosis, and we have meditated on where God might be calling us. And we have celebrated the transformation that is available to us by virtue of our baptism. This chapter ties all of these themes together as we look at how we might grow spiritually from the Rite of Reconciliation. We will develop a blueprint of sorts for living out the resurrected future that is our gift and responsibility as ambassadors of Christ and ministers of reconciliation, as Paul writes.

As we discussed last chapter, the true gift of reconciliation is not simply the fact that we are set free from the prison that is sin but also that this process of reconciliation resurrects our whole life. We have been invited to live a life that joins with God in the redemptive and creative work in the world, responding in faith to where Jesus has led—and is leading.

Yet this invitation to a full and holy life may seem daunting since God is asking us to be the ambassadors and ministers to the world in God's name. How on earth are we supposed to know what to do with that awesome responsibility?! Thankfully, we have already been given guidance from Jesus who gave us the Great Commission. In Matthew 28:16-20, we read,

> Now the eleven disciples went to Galilee, to the mountain to which Jesus had directed them. When they saw him, they worshiped him; but some doubted. And Jesus came and said to them, "All authority in heaven and on earth has been given to me. Go therefore and make disciples of all nations, baptizing them in the name of the Father and of the Son and of the Holy Spirit, and teaching them to obey everything that I have commanded you. And remember, I am with you always, to the end of the age."

In these words of Jesus, we find our call to be ambassadors and ministers of reconciliation—and what this entails. As people who have been resurrected to new life through Christ, we must be ambassadors for Christ, going out into the world and telling other people about his love. And talking about Christ isn't enough: We are called to also usher people into this new kind of life experienced at baptism—to help them live in a new way, following the teachings of Jesus. This is the ministry of reconciliation—being reconciled with God in Christ, with ourselves, and with others. It is important to note that Jesus gives this commission as part of his resurrected reality. That is, Jesus gives this commission to his disciples after he has been raised from the dead and is the New Creation.

> We are called to usher people into this new kind of life experienced at baptism—to help them live in a new way, following the teachings of Jesus.

So how do we live into this commissioning? We must actively discern how to answer this call in a way that is both mindful of the weighty responsibility as well as expressive of its surpassing joy.

In our last chapter, we journeyed into the possible future of the resurrected life—discerning what is freed within us so that we might live as God intends for us to live. We were given a vision of not only what it might look like but also what steps it might take to get us there. In the Great Commission, Jesus tells us that he will be with us always. He will not abandon us when we need guidance and clarity on how to live as his ambassadors in the world. We can have faith that our call to action will not be shrouded in mystery and veiled from our knowledge.

When we enter into the grace of God and move from sin to life, we can see the Holy Spirit begin to transform us, and we start to grow into the full stature of Christ. One way to understand this transformation is by comparing the evil intentions that Jesus articulates in Mark with the peace typified by Paul's list of the fruit of the Spirit (from Galatians 5:22-24). For example, we move from malice to goodness, indecency to gentleness, envy to self-control. *See Appendix D for a chart, page 139.*

We are able to take faithful next steps toward this vision of resurrected life. This chapter's work (and indeed the work of our life) is to explore ways we can specifically be attentive to our call, including partaking in the Rite of Reconciliation of a Penitent. We are called to use our whole self—body, mind, and soul—in service and love of God, and we must use all our gifts, imagination, and creativity to truly live as new creations. We are called to put flesh on the things that we have been given to do by God.

When we take all the graces and gifts that we have been given through the reconciliation that God gives us in Christ, when we empty ourselves of all the pride that is not in service to God, and when we take steps to live as new creations, we will know the joy and fullness of life that God has always intended for us.

# Response

In the call to resurrected life we are invited to participate in God's New Creation. However, to know how to fully live into this call, we need to do some further discernment work. As we seek the guidance of the Holy Spirit, we will brainstorm together our faithful next steps toward a resurrected life.

1. Begin with prayer. Ask the Holy Spirit to move over the waters of your creativity and stir up any new visions of calls that you want to be attentive to.

2. Keep the icon or image that you created in the last chapter before you as you work. This will give you a concrete vision of where you want to end up and keep you from feeling like you are starting from scratch.

3. Identify key steps that you need to accomplish as you walk toward the future vision the Holy Spirit showed you. Some questions you might ask yourself include:

   a. Will you need a budget?

   b. Who will need to be included in this project?

   c. What changes or additions will you need to make to your current behavior or habits?

   d. Are you working with a defined timeframe, or will your journey be a lifetime change?

   e. What tools might you need to help make these changes?

4. Defer judgment. There are no bad ideas at this point so encourage wild ideas: The crazy ones often spark real innovation.

If you are in a group setting—and if you feel comfortable—share your reflections and listen to others' responses.

# Reflection

Now that you have spent time in discernment and brainstorming, it's time to write down your plan for walking with God. Reconciliation gives us the grace to follow God's will without letting sin stand in our way. Using the icon you developed in the last chapter and your notes from the above brainstorming session, create a blueprint for reconciled living (page 140). A good blueprint should name the faithful actions that will guide you day by day on this new and holy path that you and God are walking. It might help to answer some or all of the questions below as you make this blueprint.[18]

## Creating a Blueprint for Action:

- ✛ Who are the people who are part of your vision? Who will be engaged or impacted by your vision?

- ✛ What is God's goal working through you?

- ✛ What gifts do you possess that God might want you to use?

- ✛ What does the vision of reconciled life that God has given you look like?

- ✛ Is it relevant?

- ✛ Is it right?

- ✛ Is it revolutionary?

- ✛ Is it relationally effective?

- ✛ When will you begin to implement this part of your call? When will it end?

- ✛ Where/what location will you use? What season of the year or season in your life will you do this?

- What support and resources do you need?

- Consider making a private confession as your first step in this whole processs. Find the joy in confession by partaking in the Sacrament of Reconciliation of a Penitent.

If you are in a group setting—and if you feel comfortable—share your reflections and listen to others' responses.

Now that you have spent time learning and dreaming about the role of reconciliation in your faith journey, return to the questions that you answered in Chapter One to see what has changed.

- Have you ever made a private confession? Why or why not?

- What does reconciliation mean to you?

- What is your understanding or hope of confession?

- What Bible story makes you think of forgiveness? Of confession?

- Have you had the experience of feeling guilty? Has that feeling led you to make a major change in your life? What was it? When did this happen?

- Why is it hard to ask for forgiveness?

- How much do you think sin weighs?

- Has shame ever prevented you from seeking forgiveness?

- How can you prepare yourself to take a step in the process of forgiveness?

# Closing Prayer

This sending out liturgy can be done in a group or alone.

> Open my lips, O Lord, *
> **and my mouth shall proclaim your praise.**
>
> Create in me a clean heart, O God, *
> **and renew a right spirit within me.**
>
> Cast me not away from your presence *
> **and take not your holy Spirit from me.**
>
> Give me the joy of your saving help again *
> **and sustain me with your bountiful Spirit.**
>
> Glory to the Father, and to the Son, and to the Holy Spirit: *
> **as it was in the beginning, is now, and will be**
> **forever. Amen.**
>
> —ADAPTED FROM PSALM 51

In the name of the Divine Trinity, Creator, Redeemer, and Sustainer, let us pray.

**God, you have called us into new life and set us free from the bondage of sin to be your people in the world. Be with us now as we seek to be sent forth to be your ambassador for reconciliation. *Amen.***

## Reading

Now the eleven disciples went to Galilee, to the mountain to which Jesus had directed them. When they saw him, they worshiped him; but some doubted. And Jesus came and said to them, "All authority in heaven and on earth has been given to me. Go therefore and make disciples of all nations, baptizing them in the name of the Father and of the Son and of the

Holy Spirit, and teaching them to obey everything that I have commanded you. And remember, I am with you always, to the end of the age."

—Matthew 28:16-20

## Silent prayer

*A moment of silence may be offered.*

The Lord's Prayer

# Commissioning

God, we ask that you grant these, your servants, your power and your peace as they seek to become your ambassadors in the world. Keep them ever mindful that they have been born anew in you by virtue of their baptisms and that you have promised to be with them always. Let your message of peace and reconciliation be the one that they proclaim with their words, actions, and love. We ask this in the name of one God: Father, Son, and Holy Spirit. **Amen.**

Go in the peace of Christ to love and serve the Lord.
**Thanks be to God!**

# Appendix A

# Leader's Toolbox

*So if anyone is in Christ, there is a new creation: everything old has passed away; see, everything has become new! All this is from God, who reconciled us to himself through Christ, and has given us the ministry of reconciliation; that is, in Christ God was reconciling the world to himself, not counting their trespasses against them, and entrusting the message of reconciliation to us. So we are ambassadors for Christ, since God is making his appeal through us; we entreat you on behalf of Christ, be reconciled to God. For our sake he made him to be sin who knew no sin, so that in him we might become the righteousness of God.*

—2 Corinthians 5:17-21

# Group Facilitation

The transformative chapters imagined in this resource can easily be used as a series of workshops held over the six weeks of Lent (or any time), in a one-day workshop, or a retreat. Each session includes scripture, prayer, and a theological reflection on the topic. Then there is time for personal and corporate reflection, often in the form of meditations or prayerful activities. Each session closes with a group worship experience. All of the sessions are designed to explore the Rite of Reconciliation of a Penitent and focus on the themes of reconciliation that Paul talks about in 2 Corinthians 5:17-21. The form and progression of the chapters as a whole mirror the action of the rite itself: beginning with a true look of sin; moving into a deeper understanding of guilt and shame; practicing Christ-like emptying of those things that keep us out of union with God, neighbor, and self; discerning the call of new life; listening to God's call of action as new creations free from our burdens; and then giving thanks for God's grace.

Each session can be modified for time by making the worship opportunity shorter or simply using one of the prayers rather than a whole service.

At the conclusion of the series, I recommend the group engage in a powerful "station style" worship service. This draws all of the themes of the workshops together. Those instructions can be found in this section of the Appendix, under the "Station Worship" heading. Make sure that opportunities to schedule private confession are offered, as many will feel moved to partake in the rite.

It is recommended that participants have their own copies of this workbook. Having their own copy will provide each participant access to the information for further reference, to read before the session or review afterward, and to take notes as they move through this journey of reconciliation. The book also provides enough background material that leaders who are initially not familiar with the Rite of Reconciliation have the tools to facilitate a group. The workbook also serves as a valuable journaling tool that individuals can refer to as a possible guide while making their own private confession.

These pages offer an overview of each session, including the preparation and materials needed.

The following might be helpful boilerplate as you begin to advertise this program in your church:

### Joy in Confession Workshop/Class

"So if anyone is in Christ, there is a new creation: everything old has passed away; see, everything has become new! All this is from God, who reconciled us to himself through Christ, and has given us the ministry of reconciliation; that is, in Christ God was reconciling the world to himself, not counting their trespasses against them, and entrusting the message of reconciliation to us." — 2 Corinthians 5:17-20

How often in your life have you felt weighed down by sin? Have you known the prison of shame and guilt and crave to be free of them? Do you have a hard time believing that you are ever truly forgiven of a sin?

If so, please join us on *(date/time/location)* for a unique *workshop/class* on the topic of reconcilation. In this *workshop/class*, we will explore the desire that God has for us to be free from the pain and brokenness of a life weighed down by sin. We will experience prayer and therapeutic meditations to help release these sins and be reconciled back to God. And we will design a living blueprint for tangible ways to live a resurrected life as a new creation.

Don't miss this life-changing experience!

**WORKSHOP ONE:**

# Introduction to Reconciliation of a Penitent and Reconciliation in the Bible and *The Book of Common Prayer*

Materials needed:

- Individual copies of this workbook

- Copies of *The Book of Common Prayer* and Bibles for reference

- Writing utensils

- Paper and envelopes for letter exercise (Worksheet available in Resources section)

The first common theme explored is the general lack of knowledge about the Rite of Reconciliation of a Penitent. Many participants may not be aware that Episcopalians even have a form of private confession. And even among those who do, some have distinctly negative reactions to the rite. Yet, at its core, the Rite of Reconciliation reflects a deep and abiding trust in the grace and mercy of God's love and forgiveness. This first class includes:

- An introduction to confession and what to expect while making a confession.

- Response: Write a letter-to-yourself exercise

- Reflection Questions: Encourage participants to examine their own personal beliefs about reconciliation, the sacrament, and what role it could play in their spiritual lives.

- Opening and Closing Prayers

# WORKSHOP TWO:

## Sin

Materials needed:

- Individual copies of this workbook

- Copies of *The Book of Common Prayer* and Bibles for reference

- Paper and art supplies for faith timeline exercise (Worksheet available in Resources section)

- Shallow container of sand or coffee filters and washable markers

- Soft music to play during faith timeline exercise (recommended)

Sin is a loaded word. While it can take many forms, at the fundamental level, sin is anything that separates us from the love of God. This section includes:

- A brief look at the history of sin and our understanding of it

- Response: Faith timeline exercise

- Reflection questions

- Opening and closing prayers

**WORKSHOP THREE:**

# Shame, Guilt, and Joy

Materials needed:

- Individual copies of this workbook

- Copies of *The Book of Common Prayer* and Bibles for reference

- Paper and art supplies for heart response (Worksheets available in Resources section)

- Soft music to play during prayer exercise (recommended)

One of the impediments to seeking reconciliation is the prevalence of guilt and shame that people feel because of their sins. Exploring guilt and shame is important to understanding the path to forgiveness—and to joy. Workshop three includes:

- An explanation of the psychological understanding of shame and guilt

- The biblical understanding of guilt and shame

- Response: Art therapy meditation to help begin to relieve feelings of shame

- Reflection questions

- Evening worship that includes physical movements to relieve some of the physiological effects of shame

## WORKSHOP FOUR:

# Forgiveness, Kenosis, and Release

Materials needed:

- Individual copies of this workbook

- Copies of *The Book of Common Prayer* and Bibles for reference

- Writing utensils

- Soft music to play during reflection time (recommended)

- Paper or plastic bowls (to place a picture or symbol that represents themselves) and strips of paper (to write the things that cover up that image). (Worksheet available in Resources section)

Another theme that arises when we explore reconciliation is the intersection of forgiveness and kenosis. Many people describe guilt as being "heavy." Conversely, forgiveness is often described as an emptying or a feeling of lightness that arrives after the weight of a transgression is forgiven. These feelings are no coincidence—they are naming the joy-filled reality of kenosis, or emptying, that takes place for us in Jesus' sacrifice on the cross. The term kenosis derives from a Greek word found in Paul's letter to the Philippians, in chapter 2, verses 5-11. This workshop includes:

- Introductions to the feeling of kenosis found in reconciliation and to the renewing work of the Holy Spirit

- Response exercise: Grace of Kenosis

- Reflection questions

- Evening worship including a "Letting Go" meditation

# WORKSHOP FIVE:

# Resurrection and Incarnation

Materials needed:

- Individual copies of this workbook

- Copies of *The Book of Common Prayer* and Bibles for reference

- Writing utensils

- Paper and art supplies for exercises (Worksheets available in Resources section)

- Stones (optional)

The fifth workshop marks a shift in the course as the group moves past the broken parts of their lives and relationships into the "new creation" realm of reconciliation that Paul talks about in his second letter to the Corinthians. This session creates space for the group to contemplate a future built on reconciliation and forgiveness.

Tools to envision the reality to which God might be calling us:

- A discussion of life as a new creation

- Response: Stepping stones exercise

- Discussion questions and creating an icon of the future

- Evening worship including "Walk into the Future" meditation

## WORKSHOP SIX:

# Growth from Forgiveness

Materials needed:

- Individual copies of this workbook

- Copies of *The Book of Common Prayer* and Bibles for reference

- Writing utensils

- Paper and art supplies for blueprint exercise (Worksheet available in Resources section)

In this final session, the group will spend a great deal of time brainstorming and working on what these newly created lives could look like, making a spiritual blueprint to make the action plans a reality. These questions will hopefully generate some deep reflection and interesting discussion. To help participants engage in the reality of this resurrected life, this session helps participants develop tangible action plans. The session includes:

- A discussion of what it means to live as a "new creation"

- Response: Brainstorming and discussion questions

- Reflection: Develop Blueprint for the Future

- Closing worship

# Station Worship

One of the most important things Christians can do as created beings of God is to come together in worship. Having a chance to worship together as a group invites people to be in honest conversation with themselves and with God, trusting in the goodness of God's mercy. While the Rite of Reconciliation for a Penitent is a private and individual experience (with a clergy confessor), worshiping in a group is a powerful and important experience.

Many participants say station worship is a high point of the course. Lingering doubts that some people may still harbor about whether they can be truly freed from the bonds of sin, guilt, and shame seem to melt away during this worship experience. It becomes a pathway to reconciling the hope and the belief of the resurrection in the hearts of those who joined.

This experience includes:

- Six worship stations set up around a large room. Participants are invited to move through each station at their own pace and as they feel called. Each station is designed to focus on a topic explored in one session.

- It is helpful to set up each prayer station with a handout of the information so that people can move easily from station to station.

- A great way to create the worship space is to have music playing (such as Taize) and some beautiful lighting options. You may even have a place for people to light candles or have icons present. Feel free to be creative in making the space unique to your group!

# Description of Stations

## STATION #1

## Journal Station

Materials needed:

- Small journals
- Writing utensils

Taking the paper journal in front of you, write down all the things that you would like to tell God. Perhaps there are moments of grace that you experienced during this course (or season), and you would like to offer thanks. Perhaps you have burdens that need to be placed down in order to live life as a new creation. Use this journal to lift up to God anything that you need God to know.

## STATION #2

## Wailing Cross

Materials needed:

- Strips of colored paper
- A large cross that is covered in chicken wire or some other kind of cross that can have paper attached to it
- Alternatively, you can use a bulletin board or some other symbol for leaving prayers in a sacred place

Using strips of paper, write down names of people you are concerned about or things that are troubling you. Roll up these prayers (pieces of paper) and stick them into the wire cross—much like people place prayers on the Wailing Wall in Jerusalem.

## STATION #3

# Rock Art

Materials needed:

- Small rocks (river rocks work well)
- Copper wire that is malleable
- Wire cutter

Wrap a rock in the copper wire. You can manipulate the wire into a stand to hold pictures that symbolize for you the resurrection (these might include a flower, butterfly, cross, etc.) If you prefer, simply create an abstract design with the copper wire.

## STATION #4

# Heart Collage

Materials needed:

- Blank paper hearts
- Markers
- Glue sticks
- Scissors
- Old magazines

Using images from magazines or drawings by your own hand, fill the heart handout with all the things that are on your soul. Where are you feeling guilt and shame? Where are you feeling joy and resurrection? What does this heart tell you about your soul?

## STATION #5

# Healing Movement

Materials needed:

- Worksheet provided in the Resource Appendix, "Praying with the Body, Heart, and Soul." It may be helpful to have a leader model the motions without words.

Studies have shown that grief and shame can manifest themselves in physical ways. This healing prayer uses gentle movements (which can be done sitting or standing) to ask God to free us of the physical pain of these emotions. Simply follow the leader as he or she silently goes through these movements.


## STATION #6

# Reconciliation of a Penitent

Materials needed:

- A separate space or a different room
- A member of the clergy to hear confessions
- Candles
- Tissues
- Kneeler (optional)

Set up private space in the back of the room (or in another room) with a member of the clergy available to hear confidential confessions. Keep in mind the phrase that "all may, some should, but none must" when it comes to confession. Nevertheless, encourage participation. As we have learned, this rite can bring great joy and is an invitation to forgiveness and reconciled living.

# Weekend Retreat Model

As mentioned above, these workshops can also fit into a weekend retreat model. Simply follow the pattern of the workshops above and be sure to include a great deal of time for personal reflection. It is important to have clergy available on this retreat to hear confessions. A sample retreat schedule might include:

- ✢ Friday night:
    - o Workshop One: What is Reconciliation? (Introduction and Chapter One)
    - o Break
    - o Workshop Two: The History and Theology of Sin and Reconciliation (you may use the evening worship as your closing worship) (Chapter Two)
    - o Great Silence

- ✢ Saturday
    - o Morning Prayer
    - o Breakfast
    - o Workshop Three: Shame, Guilt, and Joy (Chapter Three)
    - o Lunch
    - o Free time—with optional time for confessions to be heard.*
    - o Workshop Four: Kenosis, Forgiveness, and Release (Chapter Four)
    - o Free time*
    - o Dinner
    - o Workshop Five: Resurrection and Incarnation (Chapters Five and Six)

- ✢ Sunday
    - o Stations Worship and Dismissal

# One-Day Workshop Model

For some groups, having a one-day retreat is an ideal way to learn about the Rite of Reconciliation. It is important to have a priest available in a separate location from the main meeting room to hear confessions during the day. In the proposed schedule below, the most important topics covered in the workbook are used as the essential elements. (Encourage participants to read chapters two and four on their own.)

**Schedule:**

| | |
|---|---|
| 8:00-8:30 | Refreshment |
| 8:30-9:00 | Morning Prayer, *Introduction to Reconciliation of a Penitent* |
| 9:00-9:45 | Session One: *Reconciliation in the Bible and in The Book of Common Prayer* (Chapter One) |
| 9:45-10:00 | Break |
| 10:00-10:45 | Session Two: *Shame, Guilt, and Joy* (Chapter Three) |
| 10:45-11:00 | Break |
| 11:00-11:45 | Session Three: *Walk into the Future Meditation and Icon Creation* (Chapter Five) |
| 11:45-12:00 | Noon Day Prayer |
| 12:00- 1:00 | Lunch |
| 1:00-1:45 | Session Four: *Growth from Forgiveness* (Chapter Six) |
| 1:45-2:00 | Break |
| 2:00-3:00 | Station Worship and Dismissal (with confession offered) |

Materials Needed for both Retreat and One-Day Workshop Models:

- Copies of this book for each individual
- Copies of *The Book of Common Prayer* and Bibles for reference
- Rocks
- Strips of colored paper
- Small journals
- Blank paper hearts
- Magazines to cut up
- Something to serve as a "Wailing Cross"
- Markers (permanent and washable)
- CD Player
- Tea lights (optional)
- Glue Sticks
- Scissors
- Copper Wire
- Coffee filters
- Shallow containers of sand
- Matches
- Worksheets from Resources section

# Appendix B

# Individual's Toolbox

*Likewise the Spirit helps us in our weakness; for we do not know how to pray as we ought, but that very Spirit intercedes with sighs too deep for words. And God, who searches the heart, knows what is the mind of the Spirit, because the Spirit intercedes for the saints according to the will of God.*

—ROMANS 8:26-27

# How to Make a Confession

The Rite of Reconciliation is a pastoral gift—an opportunity to return to God and follow God's call to new life.

Yet making a private confession (whether it is for the first time or not) can be daunting for some. Shame and guilt may stop us from feeling worthy to receive forgiveness, or we may be too embarrassed to vocalize our wrongdoings and need for grace. It may feel impossible to remember every sin we would like to confess, or alternately, it may feel like a depressing exercise that we don't have time for. We may worry about what the person we are confessing to (called the "confessor") might think of us, or indeed, what God may think of us. Some of us have negative associations with confession from religious backgrounds that stressed the sinful side of our nature and neglected to share the guarantee of grace, pardon, and new life that the rite offers. We may be uncertain about the confidentiality of the confessional service. We may even be unsure if we can or want to live differently than we have for so long in our patterns of brokenness.

Rest assured, however, that the bravery it takes to make a confession will be there as a gift of the Holy Spirit. In fact, it is the Holy Spirit that nudges us toward reconciliation in the first place and will be with us throughout the whole process. If you are feeling the desire or curiosity to make a confession, it is mostly likely God's invitation to you to experience grace and bring forth a new chapter in your life. The most important step in this process is to come to God in prayer and ask for God's guidance and support to live in a new way. God's grace is not a gift that will be withheld from us—through the Holy Spirit, we have already received it and can be transformed by it. As Paul writes in his letter to the Romans, the Holy Spirit will help us when we are unsure of how or what to pray.

# Recommended Process

The process of confession should be grounded in prayer. That does not mean that you spend one slot of time in prayer and feel ready to go to your church to confess. Yes, some people experience an instantaneous pull to confession of sins and a humble acceptance of the grace that it brings. When this happens, it can be a beautiful and holy moment. But this is not the only way to find the peace of reconciliation. Spending shorter sections of time in discernment over a few weeks might be a better option for some. This recommended process (coupled with the meditations and lessons in this workbook) offers a systematic way of taking a discerning look at your life, letting the Holy Spirit guide your reconciliation.

## Prayer

O Holy Spirit, Source of all light, Spirit of wisdom, of understanding and of knowledge, come to my assistance and enable me to make a good confession. Enlighten me, and help me now to know my sins. Bring to my mind the brokenness I have caused and the good that I have neglected. Keep me from being blinded by self-love or self-hatred. Grant me heartfelt sorrow from my transgressions and the joy of resting in your grace that has been shown forth in your Son, Jesus Christ, who died for our sins and lives so that we might know true life in him. **Amen.**[19]

## Discernment & Self-Examination

This workbook provides several exercises to help you look at your life and discern where sin has kept you from living as a new creation. However, many people may find it helpful to prepare for their confession using questions like the ones below. They are designed to help you catalog your sins as well as foster a contrite heart ready for repentance. You need to determine who will hear your confession. There are several options, including your parish priest who is trained in hearing confessions and keeping confidentiality. Other options include a vowed religious person, spiritual director, or any other Christian, though they cannot pronounce absolution.

I encourage you to bring this list (and tissues!) to your confession as the emotions of the moment can make memory unpredictable.

✛ What led you to this moment? Why do you feel the need to seek reconciliation now?

✛ Read through the Rite of Reconciliation service options on pages 446-452 in *The Book of Common Prayer*. Which option speaks to you and why? Tell your confessor which one you would like to use.

✛ What sins would you like to confess? (It is best not to use generalities or vague terms but plain and specific language.)

✛ What are your core values and are you living them?

✛ What patterns, thoughts, or behaviors have been a part of your life for years that need to change to live as a new creation? (The life map/timeline in chapter two of this workbook can be a helpful guide in this process.)[20]

✛ What parts of your day/week/life are you not true to yourself and the person God has called you to be?

✛ How have you kept or fallen short of keeping the great commandment—"You shall love the Lord your God with all your heart, and with all your soul and all your mind. And you shall love your neighbor as yourself?" Are you living one part of that equation at the expense of another?

- ✣ When do you feel deep joy and connection with God?
- ✣ Into what compartments have you divvied up your life and activities?
- ✣ Where do you feel heavy in your soul?
- ✣ Is there any advice you would like to ask of your confessor?
- ✣ What posture do you feel most comfortable taking? Kneeling, sitting?

## Confession

When it comes time to make your confession, schedule an appointment and be sure to spend some time in prayer that day. Refer back to the first chapter of this workbook for some guidelines of what to expect. You might also read the section on preparing for confession in the *St. Augustine's Prayer Book* published by Forward Movement.

## Penitence and Holy Conversation

During your time with your priest, before the rite ends, the priest may have some pastoral conversation and a helpful suggestion of a habit, prayer, or scripture for you to take with you as you seek to live in a new way. Feel free to ask questions or to simply listen and receive it as a gift.

## Absolution

At the conclusion of the service, and after your sincere repentence, the priest will grant you absolution with the loving and holy assurance of God's grace and pardon. It is normal to have a physical and emotional response of feeling lighter and grateful. Know that God will lead your heart in whatever response is right for you.

# Amendment of Life and Resurrected Living

Using this workbook, put into action the blueprint you developed for the kinds of amendment of life and resurrected living that God is calling you to.

Here are some other helpful practices that you might engage in after your confession:

- ✣ Pray

- ✣ Spend time in silence

- ✣ Read scripture (especially Psalms 103 and 23 and the story of the Prodigal Son in Luke 15:11-32)

- ✣ Wash your hands in the baptismal font

- ✣ Spend some time thinking about future steps using the visioning meditation and blueprint creation in chapters five and six

- ✣ Journal your feelings and hopes for the future

# Appendix C

# Resources for Priests

*The Lord be in your heart and upon your lips that you may truly and humbly confess your sins: In the Name of the Father, and of the Son, and of the Holy Spirit.* Amen.

—THE BOOK OF COMMON PRAYER, P. 447

# Using the Rite of Reconciliation

The Rite of Reconciliation of a Penitent has been neglected by the Episcopal Church for a variety of reasons. These include:

✛ Being unfamiliar with the rite as an Episcopal service

✛ Lingering resentment or trauma from being required to make confessions in other denominations

✛ Lack of education about the comfort that is given in confessing to another versus simply confessing to Christ alone

✛ A societal drift from people seeking spiritual health to only seeking psychological help

✛ Shame and guilt at having to confess sins to another person

✛ Feeling uncomfortable with the rite because of lack of training, understanding, or incorrectly seeing it as a fringe ministry reserved for only highly liturgical churches

Yet, in an age when we need connection, healing, and a safe place to speak our truth in God's love, the Rite of Reconciliation is more important than ever. In this Appendix, you will find helpful tools and tips to help you become more comfortable with offering the rite (and receiving it yourself). The regular practice of confession by individuls can lead to tremendous transformation both personally and corporately, as these individuals breathe new life into our congregations and help turn our churches into centers of reconciliation.

# How to Hear a Confession

Priests are called to hear confessions as part of their service on behalf of the Church. It is a sacred duty and is to be carried out with understanding, discretion, and learned guidance. Some tips for being a good confessor include:

- Spend time studying the Rite of Reconciliation. If you are unfamiliar with the rite or feel it is outside your personal skill set, you might explore some of these resources:

    o *Reconciliation: Preparing for Confession in the Episcopal Church* by Martin L. Smith

    o *Go in Peace: The Art of Hearing Confessions* by Julia Gatta & Martin L. Smith

    o *Making Confession, Hearing Confession* by Annemarie S. Kidder

- Have a spiritual director, therapist, accountability partner, or confessor yourself. You may even want to ask your bishop to have confession available at clergy retreats or other events. Indeed, if you have not made a private confession, it is recommended that you not hear one until you do so. It can be very difficult hearing a confession without having had the experience firsthand.

- Keep in mind that people may come to confession with a lot of trauma and pain—not just because of sin but because of an abuse that they may have suffered from a religious leader in the past.

- Before and after hearing a confession, spend time in prayer asking God to send the Holy Spirit to you—both to give you compassion and to give you strength and wisdom. It may be helpful to symbolically wash your hands in the baptismal font after hearing a confession to ritually give the sins to God.

✛ Understand the weight of the "seal of the confessional." Breaking the vow of confidentiality is a defrockable offense and a barrier to helping those in our charge. The confidentiality extends to the person confessing as well—never bring up the confession again with the person unless he or she wishes more pastoral counseling. The words and/or actions confessed have been given to God and forgiven.

✛ Be prepared to give "learned" and wise pastoral counsel including:

  o Be sure to have some psalms, prayers, and other scripture passages onhand such as:

    ▪ Psalms 23, 139

    ▪ Romans 8:26, 27

    ▪ Prodigal Son, Luke 15:11-32

    ▪ The so-called "Comfortable Words" that are declared after the absolution in the Rite 1 eucharistic setting (*The Book of Common Prayer*, p. 332)

  o Think about the type of penitence that you might offer, such as assigning a prayer, act of service, or scripture for the person.

  o Do not belittle things that do not seem sinful or "that bad" to you; they are obviously significant to that person.

  o Likewise, do not use phrases that may make someone feel hurt such as, "I never expected such an action from you." People are at their most vulnerable at these moments. Do not inflict additional trauma.

  o Do not shy away from asking a clarifying question or giving a firm piece of guidance if the Spirit moves you, yet always remain non-judgmental.

o   If you chose to have a person kneel, let him or her know what your body language will be beforehand—especially if you do not face the person directly and choose to sit with your ear turned to him or her. This position is recommended as it gives people the option of whether to maintain eye contact.

# How to Encourage the Rite of Reconciliation in Your Congregation

Offer as many invitations and opportunities to practice reconciliation—both in the Rite of Reconciliation and in less formal venues— as possible. Recalling the importance of creating safe spaces for vulnerable and Christ-like sacred storytelling, it is worth looking into several forms of reconciliation since some people may be too intimidated, traumatized, or unknowledgeable about the use of the Rite of Reconciliation, especially initially. Some ways to increase familiarity and the comfort level with the practice of reconciliation include:

✢ Increasing the amount of preaching and teaching that you do about the subject. This workbook offers several models for teaching and forming people around reconciliation.

✢ Hosting art and musical workshops or worship experiences that allow participants to express thoughts and feelings that may not yet have verbal expression. For example, art therapy teaches that even the colors one chooses can tell us something about the subconscious.[21]

✢ Offering prayer activities that engage the body (such as yoga or a labyrinth). Mounting evidence suggests that when a person holds onto guilt and shame, they are affected in physiological ways, impacting bodily health as well as the mind and spirit.[22]

✢ Teaching discipleship classes with a focus on scholarship, theology, and worship to introduce the value and importance of the rite.

✣ Using the liturgical seasons to highlight the theological and pastoral opportunity of the rite. A congregation might decide to offer the Rite of Reconciliation during Lent, for example, and present a sermon or newsletter article to invite and explain the tradition. If your church has a tradition on Maundy Thursday of a prayer vigil through the night, consider posting a clergy member in the church for some (or all) of those hours to hear confessions. Clergy can hear confessions in his or her office if the church is in use for the vigil. This is a particularly sacred moment and one that often leads people to deep contemplation and a willingness to address their own sins. It may be helpful to bring in outside clergy from time to time to hear confessions. This allows congregants an alternative to confessing their sins to a priest they like and spend time with. It is especially important to talk about the grace that comes from reconciliation in Eastertide. All too often, the Church spends Lent dwelling on the theological nature of the cross and fails to give the same attention to the fifty days of Eastertide and the joy of the resurrection and new life.

✣ Engaging in ecumenical conversations about reconciliation with other traditions. The increase of ecumenical relationships since the 1970s has helped to raise the profile of reconciliation in the wider church. Additional conversations could result in sharing of resources and worship opportunities around this topic.

✣ Using the 12 Steps of Alcoholics Anonymous as a personal exercise in reconciliation—specifically steps 2-10, which deal with understanding our relationship with God (humility) as well as taking an inventory of wrongs we have done (sin) and how we can make amends for them. Since, sin can, at times, have an addictive quality, this inventory can be a powerful exercise for anyone, even those who are not struggling with a substance addiction.

These steps include:[23]

o Made a searching and fearless moral inventory of ourselves.

o Admitted to God, to ourselves and to another human being the exact nature of our wrongs.

o Were entirely ready to have God remove all these defects of character.

o Humbly asked God to remove our shortcomings.

o Made a list of all persons we had harmed, and became willing to make amends to them all.

o Made direct amends to such people wherever possible, except when to do so would injure them or others.

o Continued to take personal inventory and when we were wrong promptly admitted it.

# Appendix D

# Resources for Participants

*Have mercy on me, O God, according to your loving-kindness; in your great compassion blot out my offenses. Wash me through and through from my wickedness, and cleanse me from my sin. For I know my transgressions only too well, and my sin is ever before me.*
*Holy God, Holy and Mighty, Holy Immortal One, have mercy upon us.*

—*THE BOOK OF COMMON PRAYER*, p.449

# A Letter to Me

# Key Decisions Timeline

# Wash Away My Sins

# Heal My Heart

# Calendar of Healing

| Sunday | Monday | Tuesday | Wednesday | Thursday | Friday | Saturday |
| --- | --- | --- | --- | --- | --- | --- |
|  |  |  |  |  |  |  |

# Praying with the Body, Heart, and Soul

This liturgy is taken from *Praying with the Body* by Roy DeLeon. Since guilt and shame can be physically manifest in our lives, let us join in this time of prayer to ask God to free us from this burden—body, heart, and soul.

**Hear me, O Merciful One**.
> *Inhale: Quietly express your prayer with your body, heart, and soul*

**Clear my conscience in your love.**
> *Exhale: Breathe out guilt, regrets, shame, and blame.*

**Your truth permeates my whole being.**
> *Inhale: With an open heart, inhale God's truth.*

**Your wisdom fills my heart.**
> *Exhale: Bowing down, thank God for the wisdom to know love from fear.*

**Fill me with your loving Spirit;**
> *Inhale: Be inspired, renewed, and revitalized as you inhale.*

**Cleanse my heart of wrath, greed, and gluttony.**
> *Exhale: Feel lightened, emptied, and open for God's love.*

**Rid my lips of lies and deceit, O God.**
> *Inhale: Lift your chin, soften your lips, open your mouth to receive goodness, truth and beauty.*

**Let them instead declare your love.**
> *Exhale: Bow your head to the love that never fails.*

**Accept and heal my broken spirit;**
> *Inhale: Look up and offer your soul for comfort and healing.*

**Teach me to be humble of heart.**
> *Exhale: Be the child of God that you are: loved, loving, and lovable.*

# Grace of Kenosis

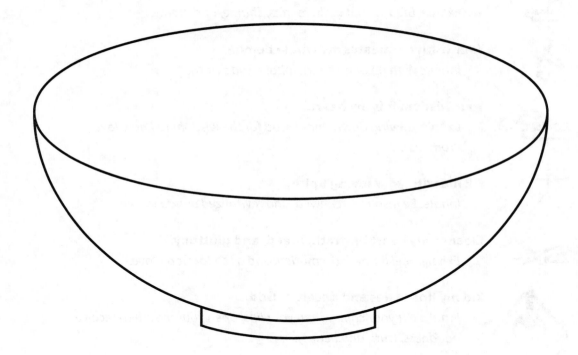

# Stepping Stones

# Icon: God's Vision for Me

# Reconciliation:
# Moving Toward the
# Light of the World

| Anxiety | $\longrightarrow$ | Peace |
|---|---|---|
| Jesus' list of evil intentions (MARK 7:20-23) | | Paul's list of fruit of the Spirit (GALATIANS 5:22-24) |
| Fornication | | Love |
| Theft | | Joy |
| Murder | | Peace |
| Adultery | | Patience |
| Avarice | | Kindness |
| Malice | | Goodness |
| Deceit | | Trustfulness |
| Indecency | | Gentleness |
| Envy | | Self-Control |
| Slander | | |
| Pride | | |
| Folly | | |

*Thanks to Charles E. Harris for developing this chart.*

# Blueprint:
# Walking God's Plan

# Endnotes

# Endnotes

## INTRODUCTION

1. Malcolm Young, "Chapter Four: Personal, Intimate, Authentic, Incarnate: A Theology of Reconciliation," in *Ambassadors for God: Envisioning Reconciliation Rites for the 21st Century: Liturgical Studies Five*, ed. Jennifer M. Phillips (New York: Church Publishing Incorporated, 2012) p. 44-45.

2. Nicole Valtorta of the University of York, cited in *The New York Times*, May 6, 2016.

3. L. Gregory Jones, *Embodying Forgiveness: A Theological Analysis* (Grand Rapids, MI: William B. Eerdmans Publishing Company, 1995) p. 129.

## CHAPTER 2

4. William K. Gilders, *Sacrifice in Ancient Israel*, Society of Biblical Literature, 2016.

5. Ian Bradly, "Sacrifice," *The Oxford Companion to Christian Thought*, Adrian Hastings, Ed. (Oxford University Press, Oxford, et. al, 2000) p. 640.

6. Neil Alexander, "Under the Mercy: Liturgical Patterns of Reconciliation through the Centuries," *Ambassadors for God: Envisioning Reconciliation Rites for the 21st Century: Liturgical Studies Five*, Jennifer M. Phillips, Ed. for the Standing Commission on Liturgy and Music (Church Publishing, New York, 2010) p. 5.

7. Ibid, p. 7.

8. Saint Finnian of Clonard. "The Penitential of Finnian," *Medieval Handbooks of Penance*, John T. McNeil and Helen Gamer (New York: Columbus Press, 1938).

9. Martin L. Smith, *Reconciliation: Preparing for Confession in the Episcopal Church* (Boston: Cowley Publications, 1985), p. 117.

10. Ibid, p. 120.

11. Ibid, p. 120.

## CHAPTER 3

12. Robert Karen, "Shame," *The Atlantic Monthly*, February 1992, p. 4.

13. Roy DeLeon, *Praying With the Body: Bringing the Psalms to Life.* (Orleans, Massachusettes: Paraclete Press, 2009) p. 108-109.

## CHAPTER 4

14. A.M. Allchin, "Kenosis," *The Oxford Companion to Christian Thought*, Adrian Hastings, Ed. (Oxford University Press, Oxford, et. al, 2000) p. 366-367.

15. Ibid.

16. Courtney V. Cowart and James M. Goodmann, *Living in the Green*, The Beecken Center of the School of Theology at the University of the South. www.programcenter.sewanee.edu/programs/living-in-the-green.

## CHAPTER 5

17. *Living in the Green*

## CHAPTER 6

18. *Living in the Green*

## APPENDIX B

19. *Saint Augustine's Prayer Book* (Cincinnati: Forward Movement, 2014).

20. Martin L. Smith, *Reconciliation: Preparing for Confession in the Episcopal Church* (Boston: Cowley Publications, 1985), p. 117.

## APPENDIX C

21. Art Therapy Blog, "Color Meaning, Color Symbolism, Meanings of Colors," Art Therapy Blog, http://www.arttherapyblog.com/?s=color+meaning+symbolism#. (accessed November 2, 2013). Another helpful resource is *The Art Therapy Sourcebook* by Cathy A. Malchiodi.

22. Thomas Fuchus, "The Phenomenology of Shame, Guilt and the Body in Body Dysmorphic Disorder and Depression", *Journal of Phenomenological Psychology*, 2002, 33, no. 2, 227.

23. Alcoholics Anonymous World Services, Inc., (http://silkworth.net/aa/12steps.html) accessed December 31, 2015.

# About the Author

Hillary D. Raining is the rector of St. Christopher's Episcopal Church in Gladwyne, Pennsylvania. She holds a bachelor's degree with honors in religion and psychology from Moravian College, a master of divinity from Yale University and the Institute of Sacred Music, an Anglican certificate from Berkeley Seminary, and a doctorate in ministry from Drew University. In addition to her parish ministry, she has served on several diocesan and churchwide ministries as well as in ecumenical and interfaith efforts. She is a yoga instructor and musician and has many varied hobbies, including skiing, hiking, gardening, and beekeeping. She is married to Ken Raining, a librarian, and they have a daughter, Delia.

# About Forward Movement

Forward Movement is committed to inspiring disciples and empowering evangelists. While we produce great resources like this book, Forward Movement is not a publishing company. We are a ministry.

Publishing books, daily reflections, studies for small groups, and online resources are important ways that we live out this ministry. More than a half million people read our daily devotions through *Forward Day by Day*, which is also available in Spanish (*Adelante Día a Día*) and Braille, online, as a podcast, and as an app for your smartphones or tablets. It is mailed to more than fifty countries, and we donate nearly 30,000 copies each quarter to prisons, hospitals, and nursing homes. We actively seek partners across the Church and look for ways to provide resources that inspire and challenge. A ministry of the Episcopal Church for eighty years, Forward Movement is a nonprofit organization funded by sales of resources and gifts from generous donors.

To learn more about Forward Movement and our resources, visit www.ForwardMovement.org or www.VenAdelante.org. We are delighted to be doing this work and invite your prayers and support.